The Teach Like an Ally Workbook

The Teach Like an Ally Workbook

Allyship in Action for Educators and School Communities

Flint Del Sol, M.Ed.

JB JOSSEY-BASS™
A Wiley Brand

Published by John Wiley & Sons, Inc., Hoboken, New Jersey.

For general information on our other products and services or for technical support, please contact our Customer Care Department within the United States at (800) 762-2974, outside the United States at (317) 572-3993 or fax (317) 572-4002.

Wiley also publishes its books in a variety of electronic formats. Some content that appears in print may not be available in electronic formats. For more information about Wiley products, visit our web site at www.wiley.com.

Library of Congress Cataloging-in-Publication Data is Available:

ISBN 9781394381197 (Paperback)
ISBN 9781394381203 (ePub)
ISBN 9781394381210 (ePDF)

Cover Design: Wiley
Cover Image: © nathapolHPS/Shutterstock
Author Photo by Ali Vesey Photography

SKY10160249_062926

For Zade

Contents

Welcome

It has now been just over a year since I wrapped up final edits on *Teach Like an Ally: An Educator's Guide to Nurturing LGBTQ+ Students*, and it's hard to believe how much has already changed for queer educators and students across the country. As I was going back and forth with editors and beta readers about format questions and final deadlines, a new presidential administration was hard at work slashing protections and gutting LGBTQ-affirming education spaces from Alaska to Florida. In just under 12 months, schools and universities have watched as their federal funding has been pulled over on-campus queer student groups, trans students and staff alike have scrambled as it's gotten harder and harder to secure accurate documentation and affirming healthcare, and libraries from kinder through university have been slowly drained of titles representing queer voices and experiences. It's hard to say what will happen next for us, but we know it will be a fight, and we have to be ready to stand up for one another.

This is why, when it came time to put together a workbook companion for *Teach Like an Ally*, I knew I was going to need some help.

Because truthfully, I'm not in the classroom right now. It's been almost two years since I stood in front of a crop of students, trying to remember how to spell "Thoreau" on a white board sometime before eight in the morning. While I'm confident that my experiences as an educator have staying power, I also know that educators don't *love* listening to someone who isn't down in the trenches with them.

I also know that one teacher's experience doesn't always translate to another's. There are almost four million educators working in schools across America right now, and no two classrooms are exactly alike.

This has only become more clear to me since my husband Xilo (pronounced Shy-low) and I had to flee our home right as I was sending *Teach Like an Ally* to final print. As two gay transgender men, we weren't sure there was anywhere in the country that would feel safe enough for us to settle, so we sold just about everything we owned and bought a 27-foot Airstream Flying Cloud (and named her Chapel Roamin'). Over the next year, we traveled the country, stopping in one spot for only a week or two at a time. Everywhere we went, we met educators whose journeys through American education were as varied and diverse as they were.

So when we put on the parking brake and I opened up my laptop for round two, my first stop was to put out the all-call for educators who wanted to be involved.

I whipped up a survey, stuck it on Instagram, and asked for "four dedicated education professionals" who "can speak to their experience with queer issues in the classroom or within their school communities" and would be willing to sit on Zoom for a couple of interviews. My hope was to hear from at least a handful of people across primary and secondary education—maybe even some higher education if I was lucky.

I received 219 responses.

They represented 39 US states, including Washington DC and Trinidad and Tobago (I heard also from three lost Canadians).

They taught in forest schools, summer programs, the culinary arts, and schools for the deaf. They were librarians and counselors and sex ed coordinators. They were administrators in correctional facilities, varsity football coaches, and nutrition specialists.

As I read through their responses (and I read every single one), I couldn't even begin to figure out how I would narrow them down.

I then decided my goal was this: that for anyone using this workbook (that's you!), they should be able to find at least one educator they recognize—someone whose experiences hit close to home. Second, I want them (again, I'm talking about you) to find at least one educator whose experience is *nowhere near* their own.

Because this is how we're going to get through this moment together. This is what it means to "Teach Like an Ally."

We are going to ask ourselves, who needs me as an ally? Who needs me to understand and stick up for them? Who needs me to find compassion instead of judgment? Who needs another voice in the room to recognize that we're on the same team? And alternately, where do *I* need allies? When am I counted in the minority and hope for someone to show up for *me*? What can I ask of them?

That's my wish for this workbook, that anyone in the world of education in the United States (and at least three lost Canadians) finds a new way forward here. This workbook is for everyone: private, public, charter, primary, secondary, higher education, continuing education, counselors, paras, band directors, coaches, nurses, supervisors, administrators, parents, students. . .*all of us*.

We all have a role in allyship, and we all have times where we could really use an ally.

How to Use This Workbook

First of all, I'm so glad you're here!

A workbook is an incredible opportunity to connect deeply and authentically with a subject on a personal level not usually afforded to us in more traditional print. While I won't be able to talk back to you, it's helpful to think of this book as a conversation. I'm going to do my best to give you meaningful ways to connect with both myself and our 11 featured educators, and I hope you use these pages as a way not only to journal solo and jot notes to your future self but to engage your school community, either on your own or through more structured professional development. It's like Dora the Explorer, but with seismic systemic shifts in the way we think of queer identity in the framework of heteronormative educational structures.

Can you spot the courage and fortitude welling inside of you as you picture a better world for students across the country?

¡Está aquí! ¡Muy bien!

If you haven't read the companion to this workbook, *Teach Like an Ally: An Educator's Guide to Nurturing LGBTQ+ Students*, you shouldn't struggle to navigate this text, but I do strongly recommend starting there. *The Teach Like an Ally Workbook* has been written as if you *have* read through its older sibling, and there's much there that I won't be able to cover again here. *Teach Like an Ally* has a heavy focus on terminology, history, data, and theory, while *The Teach Like an Ally Workbook* will be much more zoned in on *praxis*, or the lived everyday experience and practical application of the theory covered in the source text. It's the "201" to *Teach Like an Ally*'s "101," and much of what will be asked of you assumes that you have the base knowledge covered therein.

For example, when we dive into the subject of our first educator interview in the chapter titled "Teaching Like. . .Mandy," we will explore the ways in which a substitute elementary teacher in Missouri uses crayon allocation and some easy language changes to model subtle shifts to a more "gender-neutral" classroom. What you will *not* see is an extensive explanation as to *why* nongendered language is beneficial to the development of a welcoming classroom. There are entire chapters of *Teach Like an Ally* that dive into the nitty-gritty of the history, the research, and the documented, peer-reviewed, proven impact of LGBTQ+ classroom inclusion. This workbook is a *companion*, not a *replacement*, to that text.

So what will you see here?

The Teach Like an Ally Workbook is divided into **three main sections:**

- **Section 1: Finding Your Bearings. . .**
- **Section 2: Teaching Like. . .**
- **Section 3: Wrapping Up**

Within **Section 1**, you will orient yourself within your own context as an educator (or an administrator, or paraprofessional, or counselor—remember, everyone has a place here) and dive into a handful of self-reflective activities to give you a better idea of your starting point. There's no wrong way to engage here, and you'll likely have to do a little research as you navigate some less accessed corners of your state, your community, and your own life. Take your time, and don't be afraid to revisit this section later, as your relationship to chapters therein may change as you work your way through the materials.

Section 1 is what we could consider the "windup" to the rest of the workbook. You'll get to know your state and school community better, practice flexibility and pivoting, and learn (or maybe just revisit) terminology and concepts of queer and trans identity that you'll need to be familiar with as you make your way to **Section 2**.

In **Section 2**, you'll get to meet and engage with the 11 educators from across the country who have agreed to share their experiences with us. Before meeting each of them, you'll find a short **pre-quiz** meant to orient you to the context and themes of each interview. These will help you learn a bit about the history, demographics, laws, or circumstances of each subject's region of the country, as well as some more personal tidbits that will give you some clues about what's to come.

After the pre-quiz comes the **interview excerpts** as well as a mix of **reflection questions, activities, calendars, checklists,** and whatever other **workbook potpourri** is most relevant to what each educator has to offer. Although they're called "interviews," my talks with each of them were much more conversational than they were interrogative. What these educators shared were deeply personal and incredibly vulnerable, and I tried at every opportunity to engage them as peers, not as the subjects of an impersonal study, so you'll see casual language, personal connections, and the occasional moment of joy and genuine emotion.

The point of each of these interviews is to *inspire curiosity* within you. My hope is that you can find yourself in them or else recognize how your motivations and love for this work are similar, even if your circumstances are not.

In each moment provided for your reflection, ask yourself, "What can I take away from what they are (bravely) offering to me?"

Treat these educators as your peers, and try to always assume their good intentions (as you'd hope someone would do for you).

As for the reflection questions you'll see after each of the excerpts? These are suggestions and starting points, not homework! This workbook belongs to you, and you'll get out of it what you're willing to put in. When I spent 12 years as part of a teaching team, we shared resources back and forth throughout the year with the consistent subheading of "Use/Trash or Change," meaning *use* what I've made if you want, *change* it if you'd like, or *chuck it in the bin* if it doesn't work for you. Your life is yours to create!

Last will come **Section 3**, where you'll have the chance to evaluate your relationship with the material in this workbook and your LGBTQ+ allyship as a whole. Remember, allyship is a journey, and there's no such thing as "acing" it so well that you have no more to learn. We all have more to discover about ourselves and each other, so the finish line is the marathon itself!

SECTION ONE

Finding Your Bearings. . .

CHAPTER ONE

Starting Quiz: Are You Teaching Like an Ally?

When I was growing up in the late 1990s, I was a religious subscriber to fashion and culture magazines like *Seventeen* and *CosmoGirl*. This wasn't because I had a deeply held love for fashion (the low cut jeans and cap sleeves of the era always looked like my personal nightmare) but because there was nothing that buttered my biscuit quite like a *personality quiz*. I adored learning more about myself through the lens of the glossy and slightly perfumed pages of those magazines. Would my love last? Is my best friend *bad news*? Do cliques *rule my life*? Am I the *life of the party*, or a *wilting wallflower*? Is he the *one for me*, or just a *summer fling*?

It wasn't until I was much older (and enough time had passed for the low cut jeans to cycle out of fashion and then back in again) that I realized my love wasn't for the magazines but for **self-reflection**. The writers of these quizzes don't know more about you than you know yourself—investigating inward is a skill, one that we can return to over and over for the entirety of our lives.

All of this to say: use this quiz *not as a* sentencing but as a starting point. Let this be a tool to guide your self-reflection, not override it. The questions here are meant to allow you a shot at personal vulnerability, and we are all starting from different blocks.

You'll see this exact same quiz again at the end of the workbook, offering a chance for you to measure your growth. Where are you able to **build your confidence**? What gaps in your knowledge or perspective find the space to be filled? The changes might be **vast** or **immeasurably narrow**, but the truth is the same either way: **the only way to lose is not to try**.

As you answer each question, keep a tally of your points as you go. Each answer is worth either **4, 3, 2, or 1** point(s), and the values **won't be the same** every time. **Double-check your math before you visit your results!**

1. I have made mistakes as an ally.
   A. Strongly Agree (4)
   B. Agree (3)
   C. Disagree (2)
   D. Strongly Disagree (1)
2. When I have made a mistake as an ally, I have attempted steps to take accountability and begin repair.
   A. Strongly Agree (4)
   B. Agree (3)
   C. Disagree (2)
   D. Strongly Disagree (1)
3. When my mistakes are brought to my attention, I try to avoid reacting quickly and defensively.
   A. Strongly Agree (4)
   B. Agree (3)
   C. Disagree (2)
   D. Strongly Disagree (1)
4. I see "ally" as a verb and not a noun.
   A. Strongly Agree (4)
   B. Agree (3)
   C. Disagree (2)
   D. Strongly Disagree (1)
5. The young people in my life know, because I have told them, that they can come to me when they are feeling unsafe or unsupported.
   A. Strongly Agree (4)
   B. Agree (3)
   C. Disagree (2)
   D. Strongly Disagree (1)
6. I try not to challenge the systems and structures of my school and community, as they seem to work well for most people.
   A. Strongly Agree (1)
   B. Agree (2)
   C. Disagree (3)
   D. Strongly Disagree (4)

7. There are only one or two staff members in our school community who know about and handle LGBTQ+ issues, and that system works well enough.
   A. Strongly Agree (1)
   B. Agree (2)
   C. Disagree (3)
   D. Strongly Disagree (4)
8. When I need to learn about a term, concept, or event in the LGBTQ+ community, I will ask a student first.
   A. Strongly Agree (1)
   B. Agree (2)
   C. Disagree (3)
   D. Strongly Disagree (4)
9. My students can "just tell" that I'm supportive of them, and I don't have to do anything further to be an ally to them.
   A. Strongly Agree (1)
   B. Agree (2)
   C. Disagree (3)
   D. Strongly Disagree (4)
10. Sitting in discomfort and challenging my belief systems is part of allyship work.
   A. Strongly Agree (4)
   B. Agree (3)
   C. Disagree (2)
   D. Strongly Disagree (1)
11. If I hold a marginalized identity, I am automatically an ally to my students and do not have to do anything further to be an ally to them.
   A. Strongly Agree (1)
   B. Agree (2)
   C. Disagree (3)
   D. Strongly Disagree (4)

12. If none of my students or colleagues tells me that they are part of the LGBTQ+ community, it's unlikely that any of them are.

    A. Strongly Agree (1)

    B. Agree (2)

    C. Disagree (3)

    D. Strongly Disagree (4)

13. When I look at the list of terms in the "LGBTQ+ Terminology" section of Chapter 3, I can say with confidence that I know and can appropriately use at least 75% of them.

    A. Strongly Agree (4)

    B. Agree (3)

    C. Disagree (2)

    D. Strongly Disagree (1)

14. When someone comes out to me as transgender, I can use the name and pronouns they ask of me with minimal error.

    A. Strongly Agree (4)

    B. Agree (3)

    C. Disagree (2)

    D. Strongly Disagree (1)

15. When I do make a name or pronoun error, I correct myself quickly and without fanfare.

    A. Strongly Agree (4)

    B. Agree (3)

    C. Disagree (2)

    D. Strongly Disagree (1)

16. When someone I know uses the pronouns "they/them," I know how to fit them into sentences quickly and with minimal error.

    A. Strongly Agree (4)

    B. Agree (3)

    C. Disagree (2)

    D. Strongly Disagree (1)

17. When discussing a trans person's past, I know to keep their name and pronouns congruent with their current lived reality, even if they may have gone by a different name or used different pronouns in the time period of my story. I can do this with minimal error.

    A. Strongly Agree (4)

    B. Agree (3)

    C. Disagree (2)

    D. Strongly Disagree (1)

18. I am familiar with many important historical events within the timeline of US LGBTQ+ history (the Stonewall riots, the AIDS epidemic, the election and assassination of Harvey Milk, the Lavender Scare), and make an active effort to expand my knowledge where I can.

    A. Strongly Agree (4)

    B. Agree (3)

    C. Disagree (2)

    D. Strongly Disagree (1)

19. I consider myself an advanced learner in the world of national and international LGBTQ+ cultural, social, and/or political history, and could likely teach others.

    A. Strongly Agree (4)

    B. Agree (3)

    C. Disagree (2)

    D. Strongly Disagree (1)

20. I avoid gendered language and assumptions within my classroom and school community, such as "I need a couple of boys to help me with these desks" and "let's make this game boys versus girls."

    A. Strongly Agree (4)

    B. Agree (3)

    C. Disagree (2)

    D. Strongly Disagree (1)

21. "Gender" is a recent issue in schools, and it hasn't been a problem in the past.
    A. Strongly Agree (1)
    B. Agree (2)
    C. Disagree (3)
    D. Strongly Disagree (4)
22. Staff training concerning LGBTQ+ school equity should be optional.
    A. Strongly Agree (1)
    B. Agree (2)
    C. Disagree (3)
    D. Strongly Disagree (4)
23. There is room within my classroom or school community for students to make mistakes, and there are no expectations of perfection.
    A. Strongly Agree (4)
    B. Agree (3)
    C. Disagree (2)
    D. Strongly Disagree (1)
24. I do not apologize to my students.
    A. Strongly Agree (1)
    B. Agree (2)
    C. Disagree (3)
    D. Strongly Disagree (4)
25. I am hard on myself and try for perfection.
    A. Strongly Agree (1)
    B. Agree (2)
    C. Disagree (3)
    D. Strongly Disagree (4)
26. IEPS, 504s, and other accommodation plans are inconvenient and often unnecessary for student success.
    A. Strongly Agree (1)
    B. Agree (2)
    C. Disagree (3)
    D. Strongly Disagree (4)

27. I know that issues of equity across identities, including neurodivergence, race, ethnicity, socioeconomic status, and disability, are tied together in their efforts and purpose, and they cannot be treated as separate in the fight for LGBTQ+ liberation.

    A. Strongly Agree (4)

    B. Agree (3)

    C. Disagree (2)

    D. Strongly Disagree (1)

28. I know where the closest community LGBTQ+ Center is located, along with what relevant services and programming might be helpful for my students and colleagues.

    A. Strongly Agree (4)

    B. Agree (3)

    C. Disagree (2)

    D. Strongly Disagree (1)

29. I am familiar with the concept of "rainbow washing," and I know how to prevent it within my own classroom or school community.

    A. Strongly Agree (4)

    B. Agree (3)

    C. Disagree (2)

    D. Strongly Disagree (1)

30. I am familiar with the concepts of "emotional safety" and "psychological safety," and I am confident that my classroom and/or school community promotes both.

    A. Strongly Agree (4)

    B. Agree (3)

    C. Disagree (2)

    D. Strongly Disagree (1)

31. I agree with the phrase "a good teacher is like a candle—they consume themselves to light the way for others."

    A. Strongly Agree (1)

    B. Agree (2)

    C. Disagree (3)

    D. Strongly Disagree (4)

32. I try not to hold children accountable for my feelings. It is my responsibility to regulate myself before engaging with a dysregulated student.
    A. Strongly Agree (4)
    B. Agree (3)
    C. Disagree (2)
    D. Strongly Disagree (1)
33. It is sometimes appropriate to use shame as a teaching strategy.
    A. Strongly Agree (1)
    B. Agree (2)
    C. Disagree (3)
    D. Strongly Disagree (4)
34. I am familiar with the "paradox of tolerance," and I know that I cannot establish a "safe enough" space for LGBTQ+ students within one.
    A. Strongly Agree (4)
    B. Agree (3)
    C. Disagree (2)
    D. Strongly Disagree (1)
35. The policies of my classroom or school community are constructed for the safety and best outcomes of my students, not from my own need for control.
    A. Strongly Agree (4)
    B. Agree (3)
    C. Disagree (2)
    D. Strongly Disagree (1)
36. The physical environment of my classroom or school community sends a message to LGBTQ+ students and adults that they are safe and respected.
    A. Strongly Agree (4)
    B. Agree (3)
    C. Disagree (2)
    D. Strongly Disagree (1)

37. I would support LGBTQ+ students more, but I am concerned that this is "showing a preference" to them, and I do not want to appear biased.
    A. Strongly Agree (1)
    B. Agree (2)
    C. Disagree (3)
    D. Strongly Disagree (4)
38. I have a strong handle on my values as an educator, and I am willing to stand up for them even if it makes me uncomfortable.
    A. Strongly Agree (4)
    B. Agree (3)
    C. Disagree (2)
    D. Strongly Disagree (1)
39. I can spot bullying within my school community, between either students or adults, and I intervene when I see it.
    A. Strongly Agree (4)
    B. Agree (3)
    C. Disagree (2)
    D. Strongly Disagree (1)
40. I will challenge teachers, staff, administrators, or other adults within my school community if I see them acting against the interests of LGBTQ+ students and colleagues.
    A. Strongly Agree (4)
    B. Agree (3)
    C. Disagree (2)
    D. Strongly Disagree (1)

160–140 points:
You're definitely teaching like an ally, and you're ready to teach others in turn! An expert in the field of LGBTQ+ equity, be proud of what you know and the ways in which you have grown, but don't keep it to yourself! Use your knowledge to enrich your community and help bring other educators up with you. You're killing it!

139–105 points:
You're making major strides to teach like an ally, and you still have room to grow! Though you might not be ready yet to lead a workshop on LGBTQ+ equity, you're putting in the hours and doing an incredible job of expanding your horizons. Keep going!

104–60 points:
You're on board with some of this work, but there are still some gaps in your feelings or understanding, and that's okay! It's hugely impressive to try something new, even if you don't 100% "get it" yet. I'm glad you're here.

59–40 points:
Thank you for being here! You're beginning right at the starting line, which is exactly where all of us begin at some point or another. As you move forward from here, keep your mind and your heart open. Your students will surely benefit, and you won't regret a minute of it.

CHAPTER TWO

Figuring Out Your Context

This work is different everywhere. The chasm between supporting a trans kid in New York versus Florida, or California versus Missouri, is almost too astronomical to truly quantify. And as easy as it would be to assume that knowing the outline of your borders will hand you the key to knowing your rights and supporting your colleagues and students, it really won't. This is because your specific context is made up of more than laws—it's composed of hundreds of years of history, the hundreds (if not thousands) of people who make up your local and school community, and an uncountable number of local policies, ordinances, and knowledge that you're only going to be able to collect over a long and patient lifetime.

So, as you work through this section and begin (or continue) to gather what you need to understand your context as best as you can, remember: **this is a marathon, not a sprint**, and there is always more to learn.

Learning (and Understanding) Local Laws and Policies

There are many ways to find and track policies that may impact allyship and advocacy work within your state, and luckily there are several organizations going out of their way to make that research easier.

The **American Civil Liberties Union (ACLU)**[1] maps attacks on LGBTQ+ rights within State Legislatures on their website, filtering by year, by state, by issue, and by bill status. The tracker is intuitive and the lists simple to navigate, though when you select a specific bill within a state, the site redirects to whichever state legislature website hosts the full text of the bills, which can be cumbersome to follow from there.

[1] "Mapping Attacks on LGBTQ Rights in U.S. State Legislatures in 2026 | American Civil Liberties Union." American Civil Liberties Union, 23 Jan. 2026, `www.aclu.org/legislative-attacks-on-lgbtq-rights-2026`.

2025 Legislative Session

In 2025, the ACLU tracked 616 Anti-LGBTQ bills in the U.S.

Choose a state on the map to show the different bills targeting LGBTQ Rights and take action. While not all of these bills will become law, they all cause harm for LGBTQ people.

Last updated on December 29, 2025

Bills per state

0 1-5 6-10 11-15 16+

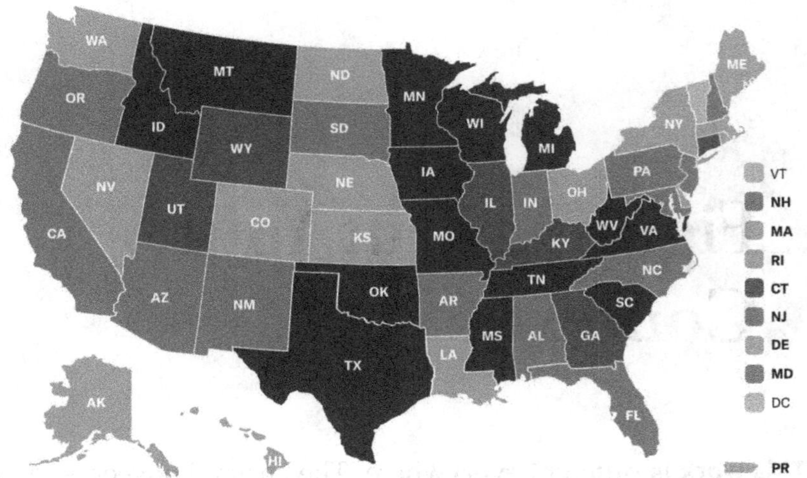

Another helpful resource is hosted by the **Movement Advancement Project (MAP[2])**, an independent nonprofit think tank focused on equity work across the country. Their map, called the "LGBTQ Equality Snapshot," tracks the same 50 LGBTQ-related laws and policies for each state across seven categories:

- Relationship and Parental Recognition
- State Nondiscrimination Laws
- Religious Exemption Laws
- LGBTQ Youth Laws and Policies
- Healthcare Laws and Policies
- Criminal Justice Laws and Policies
- Ability for Transgender People to Correct Name and Gender Marker on Identity Documents

Ability for Transgender People to Correct Name and Gender Marker on Identity Documents	Sexual Orientation		Gender Identity	
	Law Exists?	Tally	Law Exists?	Tally
Changing Gender Marker on Driver's Licenses	–	–	NEGATIVE LAW	-1/1
Changing Gender Marker on Birth Certificates	–	–	NEGATIVE LAW	-1/1
Gender Neutral Options				
"X" Option on Driver's Licenses	–	–	✖	0/0.5
"X" Option on Birth Certificates	–	–	✖	0/0.5
Name Change Process	–	–	✔	1/1
Subtotal	–		-1/4	
Identity Documents Total	-1/4			

[2] Movement Advancement Project. "Snapshot: LGBTQ Equality by State." Lgbtmap.org, 2020, www.lgbtmap.org/equality-maps.

For example, the previous chart shows the information available for "Ability for Transgender People to Correct Name and Gender Marker on Identity Documents" in the state of Texas. For both "Changing Gender Marker on Driver's Licenses" and "Changing Gender Marker on Birth Certificates," there is a designation listed of "NEGATIVE LAW," meaning that a law exists specifically to prevent transgender residents from changing their gender markers on both documents. For "Gender Neutral Options on Driver's Licenses and Birth Certificates," there is a designation of X in a red circle, meaning that a gender-neutral option is not available. For "Name Change Process," there is a designation of a check mark in a green circle, meaning that transgender residents do have the option to change their names in the state of Texas.

Overall, Texas receives a −1 out of 4 for this category, which contributes to their overall LGBTQ Policy Tally of −6.75 out of 49, as shown here:

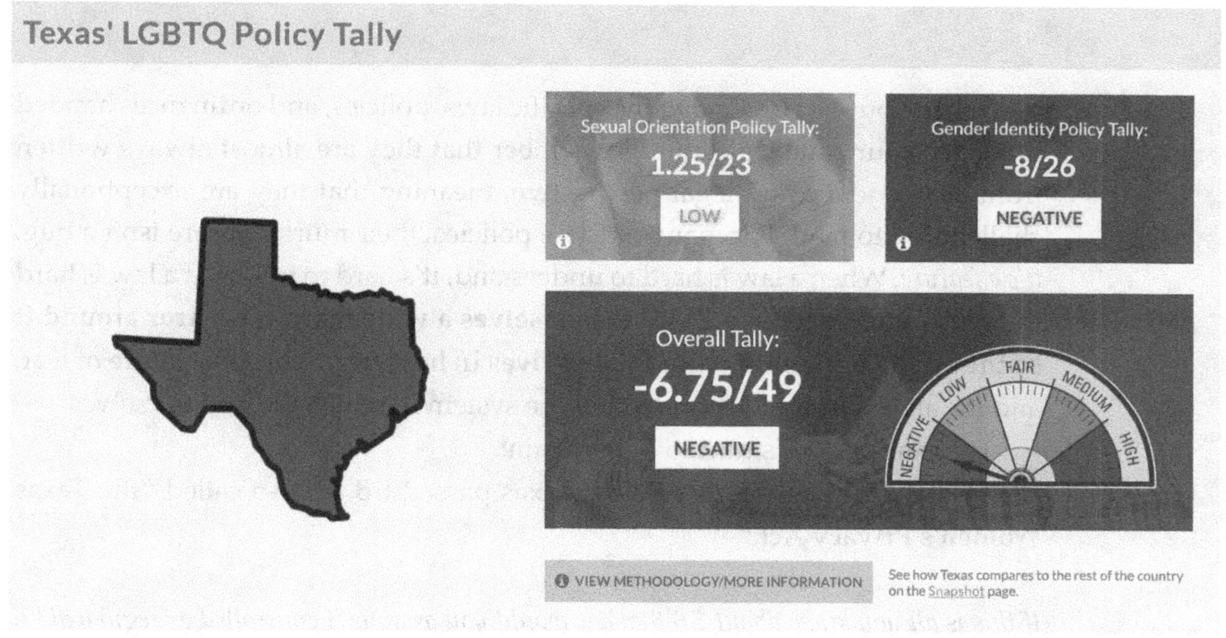

Because their data is well-organized, consistent, cited, and easy to navigate, the Movement Advancement Project is from where much of the data cited in this book and in *Teach Like an Ally* has been sourced. I recommend it as a solid starting point for understanding where your state fits in within the overall narrative of LGBTQ+ equality in the United States.

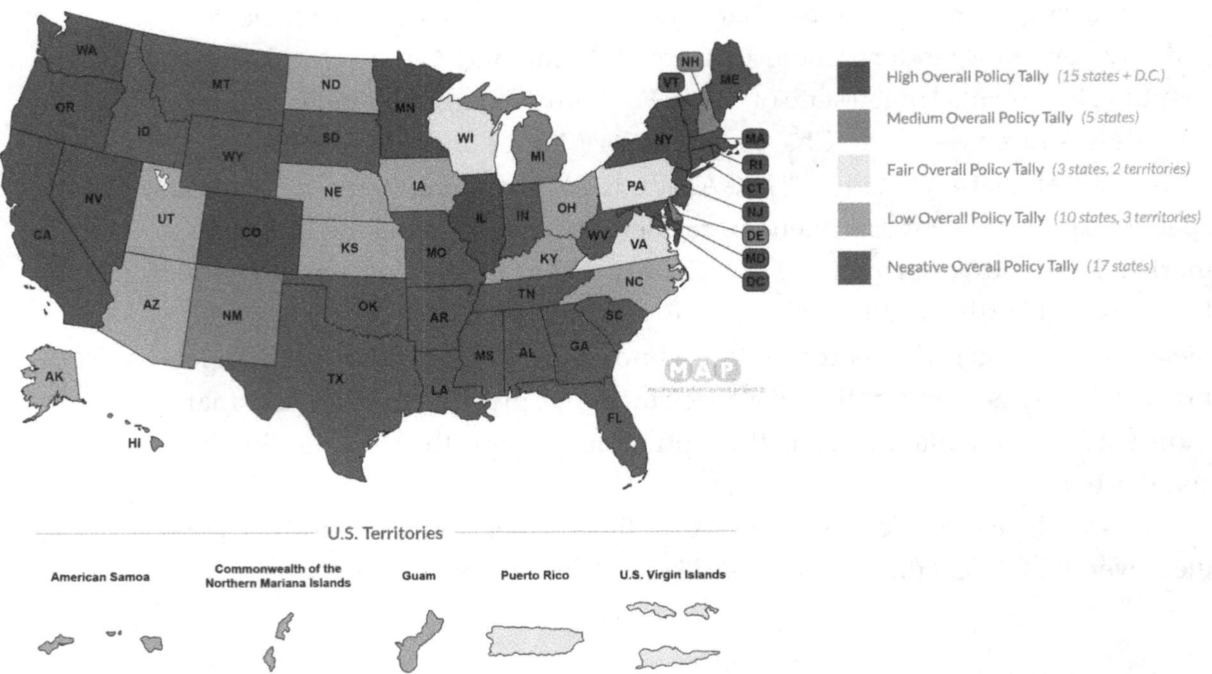

When you start to dig into the specific laws, policies, and ordinances handed down by your state legislature, remember that they are almost always written from an academic and legal perspective, meaning that they are exceptionally challenging to read. For many of these policies, their murky nature isn't a bug, *it's a feature*. When a law is hard to understand, it's hard to follow. If a law is hard to follow, **most people will give themselves a wide margin of error around it so they don't accidentally find themselves in hot water.** This is a feature of fear, and it's an unfortunate side effect of the system in which we find ourselves.

For example, let's turn to Texas again:

In the 2025 Legislative session, Texas passed **SB 8,**[3] also called **"the Texas Women's Privacy Act."**

If this is all you knew about SB 8, what would you assume it controlled or regulated?

____

____

The text of the bill goes on for just about 13 pages, and the first three define terms such as **"male," "female," "sex," "multiple-occupancy private space,"** and **"single-occupancy private space,"** as well as a **"political subdivision"**

[3] Texas Women's Privacy Act, SB 8, 89th Texas Legislature, 2025 Special Sess., https://capitol.texas.gov/tlodocs/892/billtext/pdf/SB00008F.pdf#navpanes=0.

(a governmental entity of this state, including a county, municipality, special purpose district or authority, school district, open-enrollment charter school, or junior college district. The term does not include a state agency) and a **"state agency"** (a department, commission, board, office, council, authority, or other agency in the executive, legislative, or judicial branch of state government that is created by the constitution or a statute of this state, including an institution of higher education).

The text of SB 8 then reads:

A political subdivision or state agency shall designate each multiple-occupancy private space in a building the political subdivision or state agency owns, operates, or controls for use only by individuals of one sex.

A political subdivision or state agency shall take ***every reasonable step*** *to ensure an individual whose sex is opposite to the sex designated for a multiple-occupancy private space under Subsection (a) does not enter the private space.*

A political subdivision or state agency is prohibited from providing an accommodation under Subsection (a) that allows an individual to use a multiple-occupancy private space designated for the exclusive use of individuals of the sex opposite to the individual's sex.

A designation of a multiple-occupancy private space under Section 3002.051 does not apply to:

(1) *an individual entering a multiple-occupancy private space designated for the exclusive use of individuals of the sex opposite to the individual's sex:*
   (a) *for a custodial purpose;*
   (b) *for a maintenance or inspection purpose;*
   (c) *to render medical or other emergency assistance;*
   (d) *to accompany and provide assistance to an individual who needs assistance in using the facility;*
   (e) *for a law enforcement purpose; or*
   (f) *to render assistance necessary in preventing a serious threat to proper order or safety; or*

(2) *a child who is:*
   (a) *nine years of age or younger entering a multiple-occupancy private space designated for the exclusive use of individuals of the sex opposite to the child's sex; and*
   (b) *accompanied by an individual caring for the child.*

A political subdivision or state agency that violates this chapter is liable for a civil penalty of:

(1) *$25,000 for the first violation; and*

(2) *$125,000 for the second or a subsequent violation.*

Each day of a continuing violation of this chapter constitutes a separate violation.

If you are a transgender person in the state of Texas, where are you now not allowed to pee?

According to the language of the bill, are international airports subject to this restriction? How about DMVs? Charter schools? Court houses? University medical offices? How do you know?

The second line of SB 8 requires that political subdivisions and state agencies take "every reasonable step" to keep transgender people out of bathrooms. What does that mean? What is reasonable? What is unreasonable?

What is the penalty for using a banned restroom in Texas as a transgender person? Who pays it? Who enforces it? How?

It's okay if the answers to these questions are challenging, if not impossible, to answer, even after reading through the text of the bill multiple times. If you didn't struggle to navigate it, consider: ***who would?*** Is this language accessible to everyone it affects? Could that be the point?

Tracking Changes and Learning to Pivot

For a lot of us, paying attention to the laws and policies of our state, our county, our city, and our school community is at best boring and at worst actively painful. The feeling I get in my stomach about it is akin to the one I get when I think about my bank account or the one my students definitely experience when they think about a newly updated gradebook: ***if I don't look at it, maybe it won't change.***

But we know that's not true.

There are plenty of people who navigate their lives every day exceptionally unaware of the politics that shape their world. The thing is, even if you don't pay attention to the laws, ***the laws govern you anyway.*** And sometimes, the anxiety of not knowing? Of assuming that you have no choice and no hope, so why bother? That feeling is **a lot worse** than putting in some time to get your bearings within your context, even if it's going to change later.

Being an educator means rolling with punches, even when we still sometimes catch a stray fist to the chin. As we've seen over the last few years, policies and expectations within the classroom can change quickly, and we may need to pivot when we least expect it. **Return to this section often to update what you know**, and don't assume that the reality of your context is set in stone.

So, as you navigate these upcoming categories for your own state and school community, using either the tools I've suggested or your own research, remember:

Knowledge is power, and **change is nature.** We're all doing our best to roll with it.

State History and Laws

What do you know about the LGBTQ+ history within your state?

____

____

____

____

What do you know about the larger history of race, ethnicity, religion, and gender equity within your state?

Example: history of ***redlining, social and political movements, environmental racism,*** *etc.*

What laws in your state protect or exclude LGBTQ+ families?

What nondiscrimination laws exist within your state, if any?

What laws within your state govern the rights of LGBTQ+ youth?

What laws within your state govern what educators are permitted to teach in regard to LGBTQ+ life and history?

What LGBTQ+ healthcare laws exist within your state, if any?

What LGBTQ+ criminal justice laws exist within your state, if any?

Are transgender residents of your state permitted to change the gender on their birth certificates? On their driver's licenses? Can they change their names?

What anti-LGBTQ+ bills have been introduced in your state this year? What is their status now?

District and School Community

As you research policies within your school district, they may be easiest to find on your district's web page, often under a heading such as "School Board," "Board of Trustees," or "Board of Education."

What do you know about the LGBTQ+ history within your city and/or school community?

____

____

____

____

____

____

What do you know about the larger history of race, ethnicity, religion, and gender equity within your city and/or school community?

Example: history of ***sundown towns, "founding families," segregated schools****, etc.*

____

____

____

____

____

____

Does your district or school community have a nondiscrimination policy? Who does it cover? Who does it not?

____

____

____

Does your district or school community have a uniform complaint procedure? Where can you find it, and how do you file it?

Who is on your school board, if you have one? Who specifically represents the area for your school? What is their role within the community?

Does your city have an LGBTQ+ Center? Is it accessible for students? What kind of programming or services do they offer?

____

____

____

Remember, you don't have to figure this out all at once! These are areas to explore and grow as you learn how to show up for yourself and others, and the only way to fail is not to try.

Let's Recap:

- The work is different everywhere. Your educational home is not the sum just of the laws that govern your state but the history you learn and the people with whom you build your community.
- There are an endless number of tools at your disposal to help you learn and understand the complex nature of LGBTQ+ laws and policies, and figuring out how to digest it all is an exercise in both **patience** and **stamina**.
- Many of the laws that govern our lives read like unsolvable puzzles on purpose, and misunderstanding them is part of the way we are led to feel **disempowered** and **small**. There is no shame in asking for help as you work to understand them.
- Learning our context is not a one-and-done game. As laws and policies change, we will have to revisit and pivot our expectations of ourselves.

CHAPTER THREE

Concepts of Queer Identity

LGBTQ+ Terminology

As I mentioned in "How to Use this Workbook" at the start of this book, there are some critical segments of ally work that have already been covered in *Teach Like an Ally*. It's there where you'll find a comprehensive glossary of terms (with both definitions and examples) highlighting words you're most likely to encounter both in this workbook and in your allyship work as a whole.

But, worry not! Instead of reprinting the entirety of that book's "LGBTQ+ 101: Terminology Guide" here, take a moment to look through this list of terms and rate your familiarity with each of them. Use this as a starting point to determine where you might need a bit of a refresher. And remember, language isn't a trap! As I say in *Teach Like an Ally's* terminology guide: "It's the structure for how we think about and relate to our own experiences and the experiences of other people, and being 'right' 100% of the time is much less important than being curious and kind."

As you look through this list, consider:

- Where have you heard each of these before, if anywhere?
- In what context have you heard them, and from whom?
- Is this an "in-group" term, meant for use within a certain community, but not outside of it?
- What will help you become more comfortable encountering this term again?

AFAB/AMAB (pronounced "ayy-fab"/"ayy-mab")
☐ Familiar
☐ Not Sure
☐ Unfamiliar

Ally
☐ Familiar
☐ Not Sure
☐ Unfamiliar

Asexual/Aromantic
☐ Familiar
☐ Not Sure
☐ Unfamiliar

Bisexual
☐ Familiar
☐ Not Sure
☐ Unfamiliar

Biphobia
☐ Familiar
☐ Not Sure
☐ Unfamiliar

Clocking
☐ Familiar
☐ Not Sure
☐ Unfamiliar

Cisgender
☐ Familiar
☐ Not Sure
☐ Unfamiliar

Cishet
☐ Familiar
☐ Not Sure
☐ Unfamiliar

Deadname
☐ Familiar
☐ Not Sure
☐ Unfamiliar

Gay
☐ Familiar
☐ Not Sure
☐ Unfamiliar

Gender
☐ Familiar
☐ Not Sure
☐ Unfamiliar

Gender/Sex Assigned at Birth
☐ Familiar
☐ Not Sure
☐ Unfamiliar

Gender Creative
☐ Familiar
☐ Not Sure
☐ Unfamiliar

Genderfluid
☐ Familiar
☐ Not Sure
☐ Unfamiliar

Gender Nonconforming
☐ Familiar
☐ Not Sure
☐ Unfamiliar

GSA (Gender and Sexuality Alliance)
☐ Familiar
☐ Not Sure
☐ Unfamiliar

GSM (Gender and Sexual Minorities)
☐ Familiar
☐ Not Sure
☐ Unfamiliar

Heteronormativity
☐ Familiar
☐ Not Sure
☐ Unfamiliar

HRT (Hormone Replacement Therapy)
☐ Familiar
☐ Not Sure
☐ Unfamiliar

Intersex
☐ Familiar
☐ Not Sure
☐ Unfamiliar

Kinsey Scale
☐ Familiar
☐ Not Sure
☐ Unfamiliar

Lesbian
☐ Familiar
☐ Not Sure
☐ Unfamiliar

Nonbinary/Nonbinary
☐ Familiar
☐ Not Sure
☐ Unfamiliar

Neurodivergence
☐ Familiar
☐ Not Sure
☐ Unfamiliar

Neurodiversity
☐ Familiar
☐ Not Sure
☐ Unfamiliar

Neuroqueer
☐ Familiar
☐ Not Sure
☐ Unfamiliar

Neopronouns
☐ Familiar
☐ Not Sure
☐ Unfamiliar

Nibling
☐ Familiar
☐ Not Sure
☐ Unfamiliar

Out/Outing
☐ Familiar
☐ Not Sure
☐ Unfamiliar

Pansexual
☐ Familiar
☐ Not Sure
☐ Unfamiliar

Passing
☐ Familiar
☐ Not Sure
☐ Unfamiliar

Pronouns
☐ Familiar
☐ Not Sure
☐ Unfamiliar

Queer
☐ Familiar
☐ Not Sure
☐ Unfamiliar

Sexuality/Sexual Identity/Sexual Orientation
☐ Familiar
☐ Not Sure
☐ Unfamiliar

SOGI (Sexual Orientation and Gender Identity)
☐ Familiar
☐ Not Sure
☐ Unfamiliar

Top Surgery
☐ Familiar
☐ Not Sure
☐ Unfamiliar

Bottom Surgery
☐ Familiar
☐ Not Sure
☐ Unfamiliar

Transfemme
☐ Familiar
☐ Not Sure
☐ Unfamiliar

Transmasc
☐ Familiar
☐ Not Sure
☐ Unfamiliar

Transgender/Trans
☐ Familiar
☐ Not Sure
☐ Unfamiliar

Two-Spirit
☐ Familiar
☐ Not Sure
☐ Unfamiliar

Make two lists in this space: the words that you believe you are MOST familiar and the words with which you are the LEAST familiar.

Are there any terms you were surprised to **not** *find on this list? Which other words or phrases do you believe are critical to LGBTQ+ allyship work? List them here.*

Choose one of your "unfamiliar" or "not sure" words and take a moment to research its definition. If you can, look up definitions from multiple sources. Write a version you're most likely to remember here.

Use this space to note any other definitions as you find them. Return to this space to add any more as you make your way through this workbook.

Who Is Queer?

Near the end of this workbook, you will meet Theresa, the principal of a juvenile detention facility in New Jersey. Theresa is a seasoned educator and a fierce advocate for her students, whom she loves and affirms with her whole being. You're getting a sneak peek of our conversation here, because she checked a seemingly-innocuous box when I was first scouting for educators who might want to talk about their experiences supporting LGBTQ+ students. As I was creating my initial questionnaire, to bring more intentional balance the voices I featured, I asked potential interviewees this question:

Do you consider yourself a member of the LGBTQ+ community?

They had four options in return:

- Yes
- No
- Not sure
- Prefer not to say

Of the more than 200 responses I received, **20% said "no," 74% said "yes,"** and **6% said "Not sure."**

When I selected the final 11 educators I interviewed for this book, only one "Not sure" remained: Theresa.

I have endless curiosity about the personal journeys of individuals who are working out their relationship to queer identity. I cleared my own path, but what does it look like when you're still firmly in the weeds? When we sat down for our first interview together, I let my curiosity win and asked why she had selected "Not sure."

What follows is our brief conversation before we got into her experiences in education. I'm putting it here because the question of "claiming" LGBTQ+ identity is one that is both fascinating and never-ending. If you consider yourself queer, see if you can find any part of your own internal narrative here. If you don't, see what you can learn about those of us who do. If you're "not sure"? Maybe this is another step closer to personal clarity. I hope so.

Before you read: what is your opinion in regard to who can call themselves "queer" or part of the LGBTQ+ community? Is there anyone, in your opinion, who should not use these terms to describe themselves? Why or why not?

____

____

____

____

____

____

Theresa: **When we first talked together, you asked me about the way I answered a survey question, right? Because I was unsure of how I identified. What did the question say?**

Flint: Yeah, I remember that. The question asked if you identified as queer, because I wanted to make sure I had a balance of queer educators in my interviews. I put in the option "Not sure," and you, I think, are the only person who selected it.

Theresa: **Yes! So after that call, maybe a day later, I had a therapy appointment.**

Flint: Love that, yeah.

Theresa: **I talked to her about the fact that you had, sort of, given me permission to use the term "queer," and she helped me figure out what my hesitation was with using that term. I've had the privilege of "passing," and no one's ever questioned [my sexual orientation] before. I haven't had to endure a lot of the things that other people have had to endure. So, I almost feel like I haven't earned it. Do you know what I mean?**

Flint: I love talking with people about whether or not they consider themselves "queer" or "trans," because as an English teacher, as someone who has dedicated my life to this combination of linguistics and identity work, that really hits my buzzer.

Theresa: **[laughs]**

Flint: I remember feeling this way about the word "trans" when I was identifying as nonbinary. I hadn't done any sort of medical transition, and I hadn't even really changed any pronouns, and I was always asking myself, "Do I get to call myself trans even though I haven't had to endure what others have?" And someone I was talking to at the time asked me why I was synthesizing the queer experience down to suffering. They asked me, "Why do you have to suffer in order to be queer? Why does pain have to be the common denominator?"

Theresa: **I'm writing this down. I love that.**

Flint: It changed my whole perspective. Because if we're comparing pain, right, my experience is never going to be the same as, like, an unhoused black trans woman, right? That is never going to be the same. If all we're doing is comparing each other's level of suffering, none of us get to be a part of this together, and there's no exit ramp away from pain.

Theresa: **Thank you for sharing that with me. Wow.**

Flint: We can do advocacy work on the same team, right? We are all responsible for allying for each other. There is no group that just gets to tap out. You are always going to have to be on somebody's team, lifting them up, and it doesn't benefit them for you to consider yourself a part of a different group. We're doing this together.

What are your initial thoughts about this conversation? What do you find yourself feeling as you read it?

____

____

____

____

What is your perspective on the question, "Why do you have to suffer in order to be queer? Why does pain have to be the common denominator?"

____

____

____

____

What is your perspective on the thought, "We are all responsible for allying for each other. There is no group that just gets to tap out"?

____

____

____

____

What questions do you have from here? What are you interested in continuing to explore, if anything?

____

____

____

____

Lesson Idea

Much of "teaching like an ally" means shifting perspectives away from one-size-fits-all education and rigid parameters of personal identity. Most of us spend our young lives constructing a tiny police officer in our brain made from the narratives handed to us from our families, our teachers, and every other authority figure we encounter. We hear "You can't do that" and "You're not supposed to" well after we become the authority figure ourselves, and our sense of self gets smaller and smaller until the narrative we believe about our life keeps us from seeing any kind of possibility beyond it.

This isn't just about being queer, this is about being ***anything***.

When we ask second graders if they believe they are creative, 95% of them will answer "yes."[1]

Ask that same group again as fifth graders? We're down to 50%.

By the time they finish high school, only 5% of those students still believe it.

Consider starting this next school year (or just this next unit of study!) with a narrative-shift. What reclamation of identity might be a game changer for a student who believes it's already too late for them?

Examples:

- "Who is a scientist?"
- "Who is an artist?"
- "Who is a writer?"
- "Who is an athlete?"
- "Who is a mathematician?"
- What does it mean to be "good at math"?
- What does it mean to be "good at picking up languages"?

[1] Annie Murphy Paul. "Are We Wringing the Creativity Out of Kids?" KQED, 12 May 2012, www.kqed.org/mindshift/21152/are-we-wringing-the-creativity-out-of-kids.

The Gender Continuum

Even if you believe you are 100% cisgender (that is, you jibe completely with the gender you were assigned at birth), we all benefit from taking the time to more fully explore what gender means to us. It's never too late for us to discover something new about ourselves, but it's also an important dive into *empathy*. We can all stand to learn more about each other, so try to see each exercise in this chapter as both a **mirror** and a **window**. We're looking inward, we're looking outward, and hopefully we see more than we did before in every direction.

Before we move on, let's take a second to review some of the basic concepts we will need to do this work.

First, it's important to distinguish the differences between **sexuality, sex assigned at birth,** and **gender**.

Gender and "sex assigned at birth" are often adjacent to one another, but there are **key differences**.

Sex is physiological, and often binary (though definitely not always!). **Gender** is social, and really comes down to our own internal sense of ourselves. It's how we dress, how we feel, how we move through the world, and how we present to those around us.

How do you express your gender to those around you? Think about the way you cut and wear your hair, your body language and movement, your pronouns, or any other social cues you might use.

____

____

____

____

While often (incorrectly) conflated, there is a canyon of difference between **sexuality** (or sexual orientation) and **gender**.

Your **gender** is who you are, while your **sexuality** is who you're into (or not).

Now that we've got that out of the way, remember that understanding the breadth and complexity of LGBTQ+ identities goes a heck of a lot deeper than memorizing a glossary's worth of terminology. Words change, and it's unlikely that all of us will be able to satisfy the ever-shifting kaleidoscope of our internal worlds with the limiting framework of language.

As Shakespeare said:

> *"As soon go kindle fire with snow as seek to quench the fire of love with words."*
>
> *The Two Gentlemen of Verona*

Gender is sort of like that too. People have a hard *enough* time identifying and sharing feelings as simple as *anger* and *jealousy* and *joy* without a lot of help. We've developed tools for categorizing and understanding our emotions like the Feelings Wheel, but we expect something as personally dynamic, relationally charged, socially significant, and historically complex as gender to fit into a neat little "either/or" box.

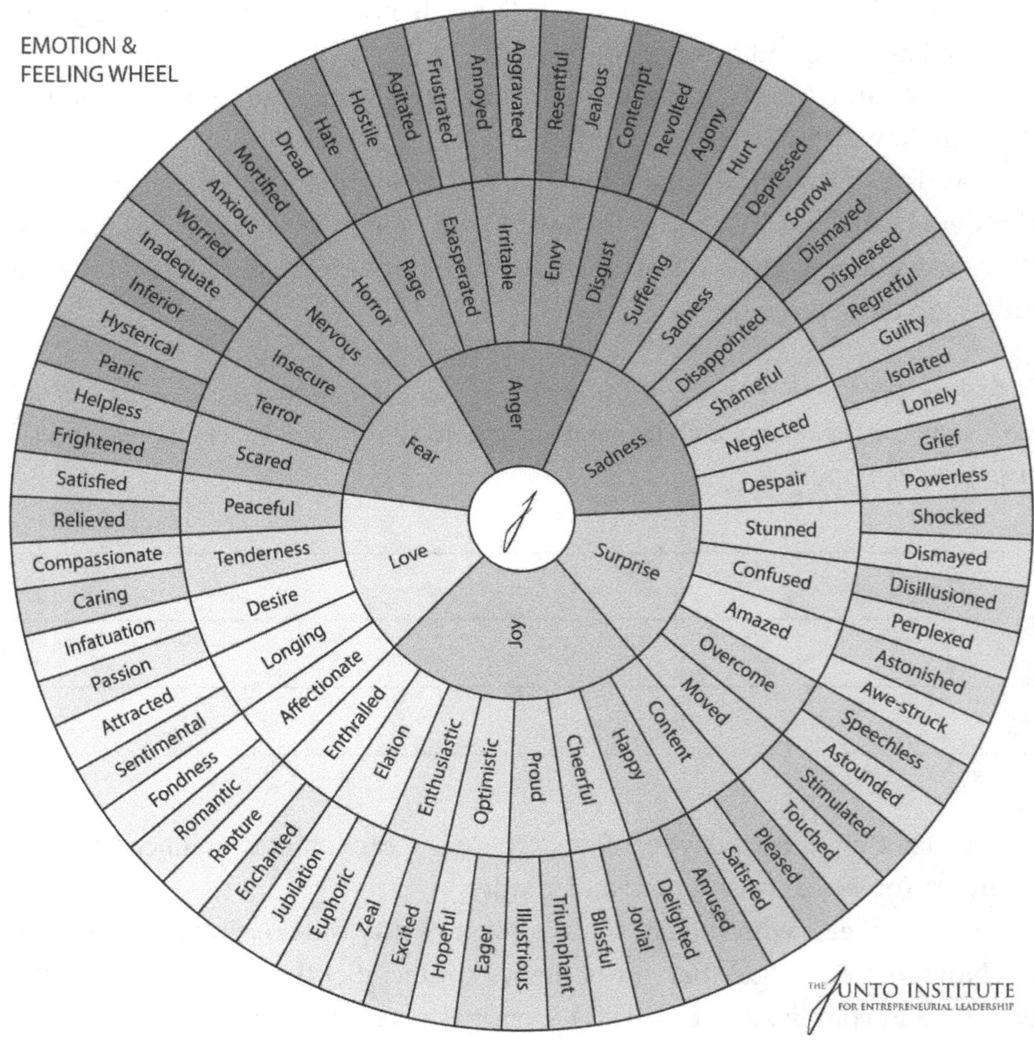

Talking about our relationship to concepts like gender and sexuality can stir up a lot of feelings we might not have been expecting. What does it feel like to tackle this conversation with yourself today? Circle the emotions that are coming up for you.

When we talk about supporting our LGBTQ+ students, we tend to make a lot of assumptions about what they know about themselves. The truth is, identity is complicated. Our sense of self is constantly morphing, and the words we use to describe our experiences are far from precise. We've been using basic human-made models for understanding the worlds of gender and sexuality in the Western world since the turn of the twentieth century, with the (likely) most famous being the Kinsey Scale.

Developed in 1948, Alfred Kinsey (sometimes called the "father of the sexual revolution") used the scale to capture the fluid and diverse nature of human sexuality in a time when acknowledging sexual flexibility wasn't especially in vogue. The scale worked like this: a "0" score meant to indicate that the subject was "exclusively heterosexual," meaning that they harbored no desire or romantic interest for people of their same gender. A "6" meant the opposite: that the subject was solely and entirely interested in people of their same gender, with no desire for people of any other gender. The space in the middle? That gets more complicated: a "2" indicated that a subject was "predominantly heterosexual but more than incidentally homosexual," while a 3 suggested that someone was "equally heterosexual and homosexual."

But was there such a thing as a 2.5? How would you even know if you were more a 2 than a 3? Could you be a 5 in your youth and a 1 as you aged? Could someone swing from a 0 to a 6?

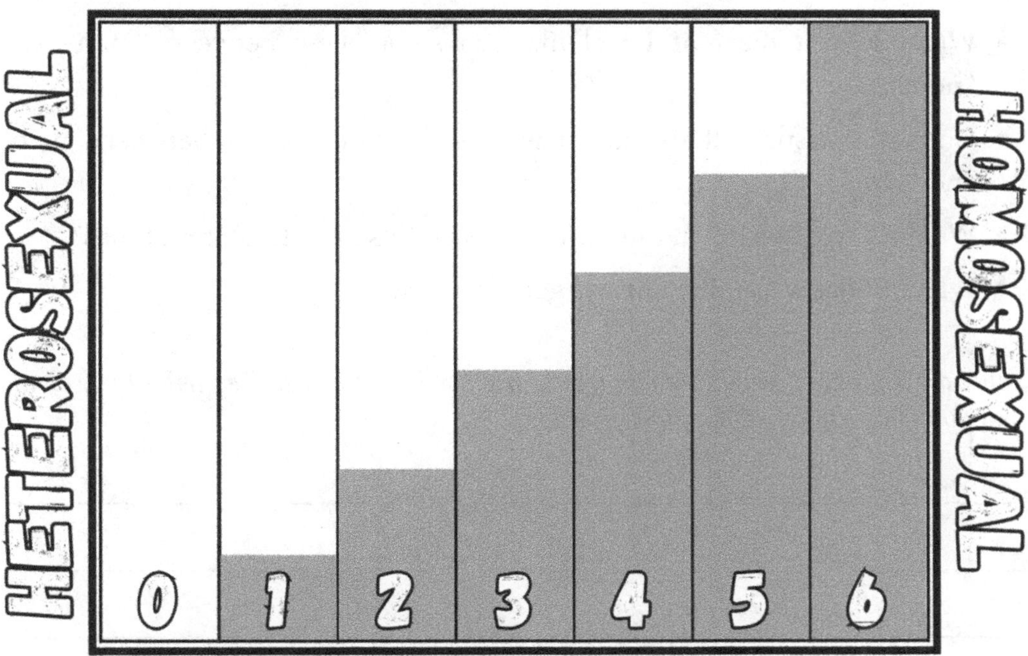

Where do you think you fall in this scale?

This is why tools like the Kinsey Scale are really only starting points, and they will always serve us best when we use them as self-investigative tools rather than hard-and-fast rules for other people. We learn best when our curiosity and flexibility lead the way and less when we believe that we have to know everything about ourselves within rigid and unchanging parameters.

So Why a Gender Continuum?

Often, when people talk about gender, they discuss it as existing on a "spectrum." A lot like the Kinsey Scale, a "spectrum" designates a wide range without clear or obvious boundaries or distinctions between values that are right beside each other, with more obvious differences the farther they get apart. A "spectrum" of gender might look something like this:

While we like a spectrum for giving us options other than just "boy" or "girl," we're still asked to plot our relationship to gender along a flat two-dimensional line, so we run into some of the same issues we had with Alfred Kinsey's tool, like these:

- What does it mean if I feel like I'm somewhere between "man" and "nonbinary"?
- Does this assume that "nonbinary" is the exact center between "man" and "woman"?
- What if I feel like I'm at multiple points on this line at different times?
- What if I don't feel like I'm any gender at all?

What are some other issues we might run into if we use a model like this? Where would you plot your gender, if anywhere?

____

____

____

____

Other existing models for charting and understanding our personal relationship with our gender still use the "spectrum" strategy but can get a little more complicated. Here's a graphic called "The Gender Unicorn" developed by Landyn Pan and Anna Moore of Trans Student Educational Resources (TSER).

The gender unicorn expands on some of the limitations we encountered with the first model, like giving us separate spaces to identify our "gender identity" versus our "gender expression," but still makes it challenging to piece out a complete picture of identity. There are some people who love the Gender Unicorn, and while I can see how this nonthreatening, arguably adorable, and comprehensive tool works for a lot of people, I'm not one of them.

There are still a lot of people who struggle to understand the difference between "sexuality" and "gender," and I don't love when these tools mix them up together. I also find the unicorn to be just a little infantile and a touch menacing, and I yearn for charts and tools with a **high degree of usability**.

What are the pros and cons you can see with a tool like the Gender Unicorn?

____

____

Enter the **Gender Continuum**.

A "continuum" as a concept is a little bit wider than a "spectrum." It keeps the same lack of defined boundaries, but adds the additional flexibility of both *time* and *fluidity*. A continuum suggests that we might not know the limits of the range we see in front of us and that we are likely to progress or change and even be in multiple places at once.

Other things that exist on a continuum?

- The progression and cycles of the seasons
- Our social and political views
- Time itself!

What else do we know of that exists on a continuum?

____

____

So here is our version of an exploratory Gender Continuum:

The Gender Continuum is an attempt to improve upon the limitations of more binary and spectrum-based models developed in the past, but it is in **no way entirely original** or **comprehensive**. The goal was to add room for an internal sense of gender along with an outward expression/externally perceived option, as they are often different from one another.

Consider the terminology used in the Gender Continuum. List the words and phrases you'll want to review before you try to use this tool for yourself.

____

____

____

____

For many cisgender people who will use this tool, the "internal gender" and the "perceived gender" icons will end up sharing the same square, either in the "man" corner or the "woman" corner—but not always!

I consider myself a transgender man, and my Gender Continuum looks like this:

When people ask me about my relationship to gender, I usually say that I am "historically she, internally they, and outwardly he," meaning that I still have a relationship to womanhood and femininity even though I move through the world (and would like to be seen by others) as a man. Because I don't consider my gender to be especially fluid (meaning that my identity doesn't move around much day to day or moment to moment), I have marked my "internal gender" closer to the center box than my "perceived gender," where most people see me and I would like to be seen.

If this all sounds complicated, it is!

This tool can be as complex and fluid as gender itself, and there's no wrong way to use it. Instead of using a little brain or pair of eyes icon to mark a spot, I've seen people use:

- A little squiggly line routing a maze from one end to the other
- Clock or season icons to mark when they feel one way or another
- A Lego brick stuck exactly in the center

Just like the Kinsey Scale, this is a tool meant to **explore**, not to **diagnose**.

Because here's the thing about our community: as much as we love giving ourselves labels, **we aren't especially fond of being handed one**. Charts like these will always be dissatisfying for someone.

If you like it, amazing! If not, here's your chance to make your own:

What could be improved on the next iteration of a tool like the Gender Continuum? What would your version look like? Draw it here!

Graphics like this aren't inventing anything. Strict gender binaries are *recent* and *limited*. We're learning, returning to, and iterating on knowledge and ways of being that predate us by hundreds (and even thousands) of years.

Many indigenous communities around the world recognize gender continuums beyond the accepted Western binary. Which are you familiar with, if any?

____

____

Exercises for Exploring Gender

Thought Experiment: Imagine that your consciousness was uploaded to a computer and your body was now gone.

Would you still be your gender?

____

____

How do you know?

____

____

____

____

*What does your gender **feel** like?*

____

____

____

____

Our relationship to our gender can be even further complicated by factors that others might not see or understand, like:

- Race/ethnicity
- Region/cultural background
- Disability
- Neurodiversity
- Sexism and misogyny

Which of these elements factor into how you understand or express your own gender?

___

___

___

___

How would you explain this to someone who doesn't understand?

___

___

___

___

Which of these elements do you have the hardest time understanding? How might they play into complicating someone's experience with gender?

___

___

___

___

When you have always been sure and comfortable in your gender, it can be uncomfortable to look inward, but embracing curiosity benefits everyone.

Consider: when trans people are seeking gender-affirming care of any kind from a medical provider, we are often told to complete something called a "Gender Assessment," where we are asked to answer a series of questions to "prove" to a professional that we understand our own internal sense of our identity.

The following questions are taken directly from my own Gender Assessment. As you read them (and ideally attempt to answer from your own point of view), remember that there is no "Gender Assessment Junior." That is, young adults are asked to have the same (secure and assured!) grasp of their answers as adults.

Would ***you*** be able to "pass"?

What is your connection between your physical body and your experience with gender?

____

____

____

____

Do you find yourself with a strong desire to be seen as your gender? Describe this desire.

____

____

____

____

How long have you understood yourself as your gender? Describe this experience.

____

____

____

____

Describe your relationship with your secondary sex characteristics (meaning the characteristics that developed in your body after puberty).

___

___

___

___

Do you have a strong conviction that you have the typical feelings and reactions of your true gender?

___

___

___

___

Do you have a strong desire to be treated as a gender other than the one you were assigned at birth? Describe this desire.

___

___

___

___

How would a change in your physical body change your life?

___

___

___

___

Remember, just like within "Figuring Out Your Context," you don't have to have this all handled at once! These are areas to explore and grow as you learn how to show up for yourself and others, and the only way to fail is not to try.

Let's Recap

- As educators, we have a responsibility to embrace *curiosity* and *empathy*. Exploring our own relationship with gender (along with the myriad of ways that relationship can become *exceptionally complicated*) helps us get better at both!
- There is no perfect, clear-cut way to uncomplicate gender. We can use tools like the Gender Continuum to **understand ourselves** but not to **diagnose others.**
- When we encounter students, colleagues, or loved ones who are on their own gender exploration journey, it's important to remember that these conversations aren't new, and they never end!

Letter Template: Coming Out to Colleagues

One of the most uncomfortable steps in understanding yourself as trans (or nonbinary!) is cluing everyone into your truth. For many of us, this is a step that won't happen right away (or at all), and it's important to remember that you are absolutely still trans even if it isn't safe to tell others.

If, however, you are interested in letting your colleagues and/or your school community know about changes on your horizon, here are a few tips as you orchestrate your social transition at work:

1. Review your state and school district nondiscrimination policies to be sure that you will be protected in the event of **employment discrimination** and **harassment**. Put nothing in writing until you're sure the environment is safe.
2. Less is more—don't overexplain! No one is owed your reasoning, your timeline, or your medical history. **Stick to the basics.**
3. The call to action is **not a suggestion**. Respecting your name, your pronouns, and your basic human dignity are givens, not favors. Try to avoid any version of "pretty please" when you let folks know who you are. You can be gentle without becoming a door mat.

Suggested template for colleagues:

Hello, team!

I wanted to take a quick moment this morning to send a note about some changes that are coming for me and the way I show up here at [SCHOOL]. I am in the early stages of transitioning and will be using a new name and pronouns moving forward, so you will see a shift in my email to **NAME** (PRONOUNS).

I know it can sometimes take a moment to adjust to change, and I'm more than happy to answer questions privately as I work on updating paperwork and my digital presence to my chosen name.

Thank you in advance for your understanding and patience, and I'll work to make sure I show up in the same way!

Best,

NAME
(PRONOUNS)

Suggested template for HR/personnel:

Good morning!

As you may have seen in my school-wide email today, I am in the early stages of transitioning and will be using a new name and pronouns moving forward: **NAME** (PRONOUNS).

Please let me know what you need from me in order to update any and all possible records and paperwork to my chosen name and pronouns.

Thank you so much for your help,

NAME
(PRONOUNS)

School-Wide Transition Plan

Within states with protections and considerations for transgender children, many schools choose to utilize individual transition plans (ITPs) to help students and families through the challenges and anxieties of transitioning socially at school.

The following is an example of an ITP from a school district in California:

Individual Transition Plan (ITP)

Education Code Section 221.5 (f) ***A pupil shall be permitted to participate in sex-segregated school programs and activities, including athletic teams and competitions, and use facilities consistent with his or her gender identity, irrespective of the gender listed on the pupil's records.***

Identified Name: ______________________________

Name as it Appears on Pupil's Records: ______________________________

Identified Gender: ☐ Male ☐ Female

Preferred timing of transition plan implementation: ☐ Immediately ☐ Effective Date ________

Level of Privacy/Confidentiality (I agree the following individuals have a legitimate need to know both Legal Name & Identified Name):

☐ Principal ☐ Assistant Principal(s) ☐ Registrar ☐ School Counselor ☐ Health Office Staff

Other adults with a need to know:

____

Teacher(s) Notification (Upon request, the school will notify selected teacher(s) of the Individual Transition Plan (ITP), so they can apply confidentiality safeguards, equal access to educational opportunities, and intervention if bullying or harassment issues are perceived.):

☐ School shall not notify any of my teachers. ☐ School may notify ALL of my teachers.

☐ School may notify the following teacher(s):

____

☐ School may notify substitute teacher(s)

Notification of class-mates (It is a personal decision to release confidential information to class-mates and/or staff.):

Identify safe friends and/or staff to share news:

____

Identify potential unsafe students and/or situations:

____

Response plan for dealing with unsafe students and/or situations:

____

All instances of Harassment/Bullying shall be immediately reported to the designated site administration.

Report Harassment/Bullying to the following staff member(s):

____

Bathroom Usage (The following options are available to protect the confidentiality of the student.):

☐ The use of single-stall bathrooms for increased privacy, where available.
☐ The use of nurse or staff restroom for increased privacy, where available.
☐ Transgender male (female/male) use a single-stall in male restroom.
☐ Transgender male (female/male) use a single-stall in female restroom.
☐ Transgender female (male/female) use a single-stall in female restroom.
☐ Transgender female (male/female) use a single-stall in male restroom.

Locker Room Usage (The following options for usage of boy's/girl's locker room are provided to protect the confidentiality of the student.):

☐ Student may waive requirement to shower for PE classes.
☐ Student uses private changing and bathroom areas (e.g., single-changing stalls with door/curtain, single-bathroom stalls, and/or private showers with door/curtain).
☐ In order to protect his/her privacy and the reasonable expectation of privacy of other students, students shall be appropriately clothed when outside of private changing and bathroom areas.
☐ Student may request an individual changing schedule.
☐ Student may consider an alternative satisfaction of PE requirement.

Other Accommodations for ITP:

____

Student	Date	Parent/Guardian	Date
Site Administrator	Date	Other Staff Member	Date

rev. 5/16

How might a plan like this make life easier for transgender students?

____

____

____

____

How might a plan like this make life easier for teachers and school staff?

____

____

____

____

What part of this plan needs to be changed or updated? What is missing?

____

____

____

____

Within states and school communities where an ITP is not possible, what other options exist for educators and students?

____

____

____

____

SECTION TWO

Teaching Like. . .

CHAPTER FOUR

Where in the World Is. . .

It's just about time to meet our educators, but first we need to ask, where are they?

As we learned in "Figuring Out Your Context," regional differences within the United States are vast, and the context in which we live and work has a huge impact on the way we move through our school communities and show up with our students.

In order of appearance, these are the educators[1] we will meet in the following pages, along with their home states:

- Mandy P: *Missouri*
- I.C.: *California*
- Sean Em R.: *Massachusetts*
- Stanley P: *North Carolina*
- Matthew C: *Texas*
- Bali M: *North Carolina*
- Janelle G: *New Mexico*
- Katherine R: *Alabama*
- Theresa B: *New Jersey*
- Ro P and Alaina D: *New York*

[1] Note: Some educators have chosen to go by initials or pseudonyms.

On a map, that looks like this:

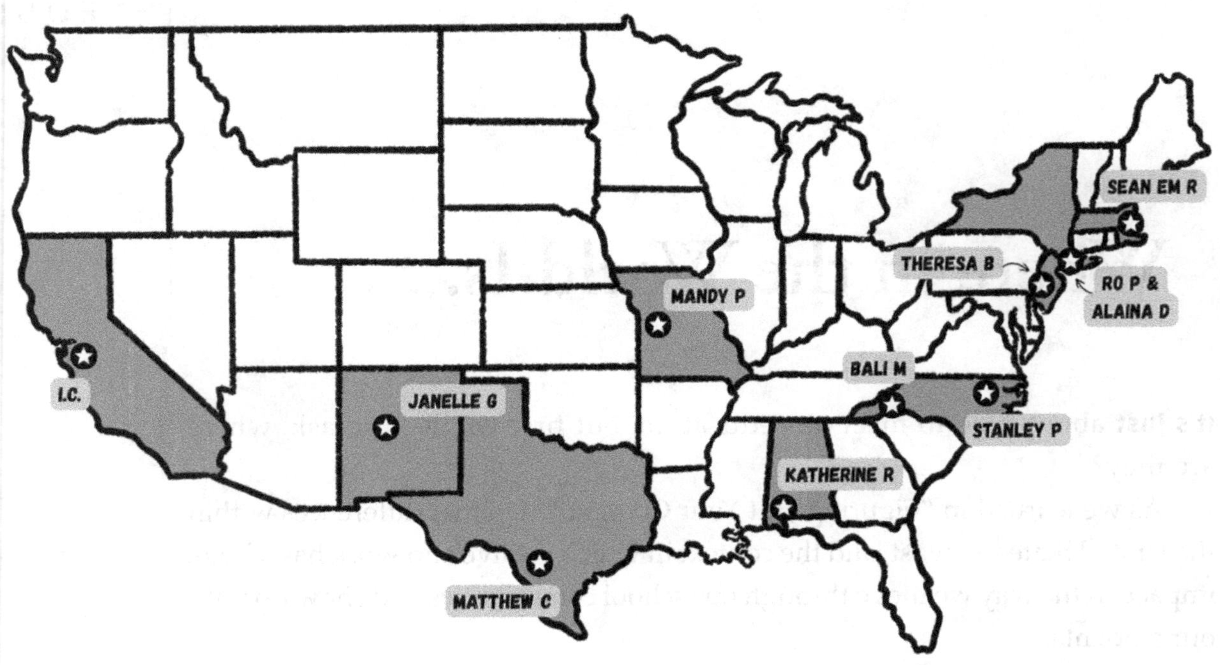

Where are you? Take a moment to plot yourself on this map.

Which educator is closest to you? Who is furthest?

____

____

Based on your understanding of regional culture, laws, and history, whose experience do you anticipate being ***closest*** *to your own? Why?*

____

____

Based on your understanding of regional culture, laws, and history, whose experience do you anticipate being ***furthest*** *from your own? Why?*

____

____

Next, you will see space listed for each of the states represented by our educators (there are nine, as we will visit North Carolina twice). Take some time to bullet point information you know or have researched about the regional culture, laws, and history of each state. What are your thoughts about how each state addresses LGBTQ+ equality?

Missouri

____
____
____
____
____
____

North Carolina

____
____
____
____
____
____

California

____
____
____
____
____
____

Texas

____
____
____
____
____
____

Massachusetts

____
____
____
____
____
____

New Mexico

____
____
____
____
____
____

Alabama

____

____

____

____

____

____

New York

____

____

____

____

____

____

New Jersey

____

____

____

____

____

____

What state do you have the strongest assumptions about, especially when it comes to LGBTQ+ equality? Why?

____

____

____

____

Based on nothing but the information you have about their location within the United States, who do you anticipate will have the easiest time in their allyship work? Who will struggle the most? Why?

____

____

____

____

Leave this answer blank *until you return from the end of this workbook. Were your assumptions correct? Why or why not?*

____

____

____

____

Without any further ado, it's time to meet our educators! Remember, lead with **curiosity**, extend **empathy** and **grace**, and assume **good intentions** to the best of your ability. We're all learning, and we all have so much to give to one another.

Here we go!

CHAPTER FIVE

Teaching Like. . .

Teaching Like. . .Mandy

Pre-Quiz[1]

1. Missouri is one of only two states with a law *preventing* schools or districts from adding LGBTQ+ protections to anti-bullying policies.[2] Which other state joins them?
   A. Georgia
   B. New York
   C. South Dakota
   D. Idaho
2. According to the 2022 US Trans Survey,[3] what percentage of transgender people indicate that their immediate families are "very supportive" of their transition?
   A. 31%
   B. 50%
   C. 8%
   D. 19%
3. Nationwide, the percentage of adults who identify as LGBTQ+ is just about 9.3%.[4] What is that percentage in Missouri?[5]
   A. 9.3%
   B. 5.1%
   C. 4.3%
   D. 3.8%

[1] Answer Key: 1. C, 2. A, 3. D, 4. D.

[2] LGBTQ Youth: Anti-Bullying Laws. 1 Jan 2024. https://www.mapresearch.org/img/maps/citations-schools-bullying.pdf.

[3] "Family - US Trans Survey." US Trans Survey, 13 Aug 2024, ustranssurvey.org/report/family/.

[4] Jones, Jeffrey M. "LGBTQ+ Identification in U.S. Rises to 9.3%." GALLUP, Gallup, 20 Feb 2025, news.gallup.com/poll/656708/lgbtq-identification-rises.aspx.

[5] Preview "Movement Advancement Project | State Profiles." www.lgbtmap.org, www.lgbtmap.org/equality_maps/profile_state/MO.

4. The average school district within the United States is reporting about how many staff absences[6] per month needing to be filled by substitute teachers?
   A. 30
   B. 150
   C. 450
   D. 600

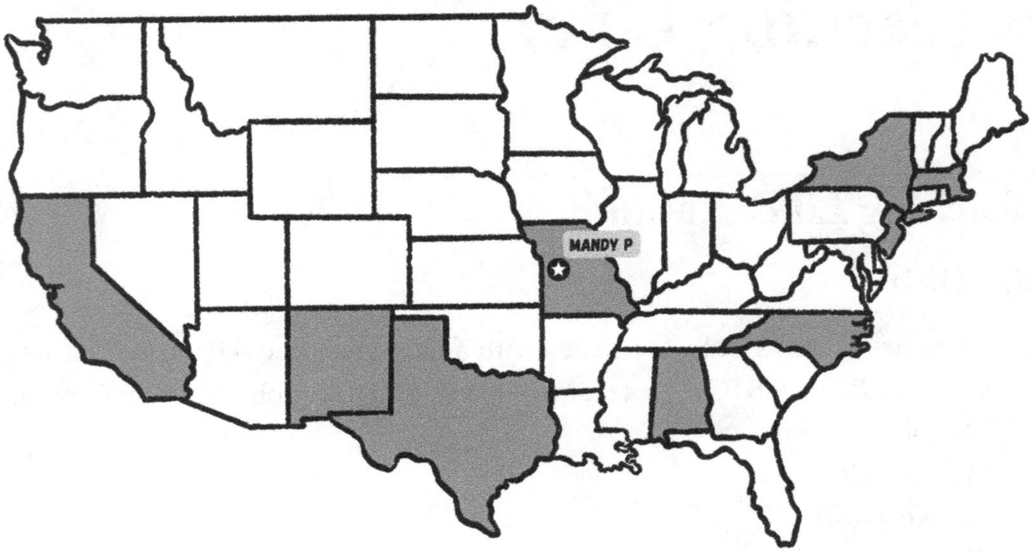

Mandy P. (she/her)
Missouri
Substitute Teacher, Primary

When Mandy was laid off from her corporate job, she decided to start taking gigs as a substitute elementary school teacher in her hometown. She'd "heard through a friend that if [she] had a college degree, it was a relatively easy process," and although her college degree was in communications and creative writing, she "always loved kids" and wanted to find a way to work with them while her life was in a period of instability and transition. Before starting in the classroom, Mandy's wife had recently come out as a transgender woman, and she'd spent three years acting as a dementia caregiver for both of her parents. So though she was eager for a change of pace, she had some reservations when she started accepting placements through a major K-12 staffing provider. "I was really kind of going in blind."

[6] Agnello, Kevin. "Talk Data to Me: Trends in Absence Management and Substitute Pools." Frontline Education, 27 Apr 2023, www.frontlineeducation.com/blog/absence-management-substitute-pool-data-trends/.

Based on your knowledge and/or assumptions about LGBTQ+ acceptance and protections in Missouri, what are some of your worries, concerns, and hopes for Mandy's experience?

____

____

____

____

In what ways do you identify with Mandy? How are your experiences in education similar? How are they different?

____

____

____

____

Pushing Back and Asking Why

Mandy: **Before I was even certified to be in a classroom by [staffing provider], part of the training was not to share your pronouns and not to ask kids about their pronouns.**

Flint: That was in the training? Right out of the gate? How did that feel?

Mandy: **Well, I had already been thinking about it, you know. Because your mind, like, you start getting excited about the idea of doing something you've never done before. I'm a very visual and imaginary person. So, I'm thinking, am I gonna write my name on the board? Am I gonna have an icebreaker in some way? How am I gonna talk about myself? And I am, at this point, three years into a relationship where my spouse has come out to me. I had three years of having gone from feeling like I was an "ally" to feeling like "Okay, now I'm in a queer relationship." That's three years of challenging orthodoxies of heteronormativity.**

Flint: And this ask from [staffing provider] felt like it was betraying that.

Mandy: Yeah, like, having lived these three years after my spouse came out, I was really working on trying to be more inclusive. I don't assume I know someone's pronouns. And I wanted to go into a classroom and bring that with me. And so, before I even had the opportunity to do that, knowing that it's just shut down? It didn't occur to me to question it or ask them "why" or anything. It's literally just, like, they're in charge. It's the system of power. They say this is what you can and can't do.

Why do you think Mandy's employer included rules about sharing pronouns in her onboarding training? What do you think is the intention behind this rule? What are some of its consequences?

____

____

____

____

What do you think you would have done in Mandy's position?

____

____

What are the potential outcomes of pushing back on policies such as this one?

____

____

Grown-Ups and Crayons

Mandy: [From her time in the classroom] I have a whole little list of things that were big for me. Like I think the inclusivity of not saying "mom and dad" is important. Not all kids are raised by moms and dads, so I used "grown-ups" a lot, and I heard a lot of other people using it too.

Flint: Oh yeah, like "you're gonna take this home and you're gonna show your grown-ups." I was wondering what you would use instead.

Mandy: Yeah "grown-ups" as opposed to "parents" because there are a lot of kids who are raised by aunts and uncles, or in the foster care system, or Grandma raised them. Language is important to me, but I didn't want to be confrontational. I like to lead by example.

Flint: Can you tell me more about what that looks like?

Mandy: So instead of saying "boys and girls," you say "kids" or "children." I would try to use "people," "individuals," "humans," that kind of thing. We should be mindful of when we're gendering things when they don't need to be gendered, because it's so much of how we see the world, in this binary lens. It's just the framework that we've been given. It's something that's just kind of like second nature to a lot of people, not because they're attached to it on a philosophical level, but because it's the "normal" thing. And the experience of now being out with my wife? People ask us all the time if we're sisters.

Flint: Oh, Lord. Yeah, my husband and I get that too.

Mandy: It's why, especially with the younger kids, when there's an opportunity to challenge gender norms, I like to take it. Crayons are a great example. Because if you just let, like, a whole table of three- and four-year-olds have a big tub of crayons. . .you kind of have to ration them. Everybody gets three crayons, and you'll hear "I don't want this one; this is a girl color," and I'll say, "Actually, all colors are for all people. There's no good colors, and there's no bad colors."

In what ways do subtle language choices model our attitudes about the world around us?

____

____

____

____

Use this space to brainstorm impactful ***language*** *changes that could help shift a classroom or school community away from "binary thinking":*

Example: "Boys and girls" → "students," "scholars,"

Boy, Girl, Boy, Girl

Flint: There are other ways to shift the narrative for kids too, right?

Mandy: Yeah I saw it a lot with line order, where teachers would line kids up "boy, girl, boy, girl." Again, it wouldn't even be from a place of fairness, but just symmetry and organization. It's just how they've always seen it.

So an interesting thing that I did as a sub is I had a little button for a 30-second dance party. You'd push it, and it has this weird German man's voice, and he says "30-second dance party" and then it has 30 seconds of a house beat. And so I would bring it, and the kids would remember it, and they would ask if I brought it. And I'd say, "Okay, well, we'll play if you're good listeners today, if you're good friends. Then, you know, we'll see at the end of the day if we want to do it before pickup." But I needed to break them into groups, where some could be dancing, and the rest would be the audience. It would be too much for them to all go at once.

Flint: Yeah, that sounds like a lot to manage.

Mandy: Exactly. And their instinct is to group up boys and against girls. So I tried to do it differently. I'd say, "It's your turn if you have red on your shirt, if you have braids or twists in your hair." I would try to pick things that were not gender-related.

Flint: It's fascinating to think about how often we encourage that from essentially the moment they're born. Sometimes even in utero, right? We've got the gender reveals that have these two teams, like your kid is going to be this or this. And there are a million ways in which we reinforce it as kids are small. It's fascinating to think about how that carries over into the way that they think about gender into adulthood, right? It's like "I am this," and then you have this whole separate species of person.

Mandy: **Yeah.**

Flint: And they have nothing in common with me because I've been separated from them since before I could walk.

Mandy: **Yeah.**

> *Use this space to brainstorm impactful physical changes that could help shift a classroom or school community away from "binary thinking":*
>
> *Example: Organizing a line "boy, girl, boy, girl" → organizing a line by favorite color or favorite month of the year*

The Desert Tortoise and the Giant Pencil

Mandy: **After a while, I had been in one classroom enough that they heard me talking about my spouse, and then they just assumed, like the kids just assumed, that I had a husband.**

Flint: So you were trying to maybe avoid it by using the word "spouse"?

Mandy: **Yeah, I tried to use "spouse" as much as possible, but then kids would ask about my husband. You're not supposed to share a bunch of stuff, but I had shown pictures of our giant desert tortoise, and my wife was in one of the pictures. It was from the beginning of her transition, so you know she was a little clocky.**[7]

Flint: [laughs] Sorry, I'm just not used to hearing cisgender people use the word *clocky*. I'm here with you, go on.

---

[7] "Clocky" is a term used within the transgender community to denote that an individual can be "clocked," or easily identified, as their gender assigned at birth. While it can be used with humor and good intention within queer spaces, it is not considered good form to use otherwise.

Mandy: **[laughs] Well, yeah, the kids asked if she was my husband. And instead of correcting them, I just thought, "I don't know how to have this conversation." So I didn't say anything.**

And much later on, I had this giant pencil. It's like this [motions in a circle approximately three inches in diameter] like this thick around, and it's got a real eraser. It has real lead that goes through it. It's wood. So it's something that I would bring to the classroom, and I would bring it out at the beginning of the day. And I would kind of use it as a bribe. I would say, "Everyone's going to get a chance to write with the giant pencil today. But if we're not good listeners, if we're not kind, if we put our hands on other people, the pencil goes away." Because as a sub, sometimes. . .

Flint: You do what you gotta do.

Mandy: **Exactly. So one day I'm at school, and the lead broke and I couldn't sharpen it. So I texted [wife], and I said the giant pencil broke and we need to sharpen it. I asked her, "Can you come up to the school and sharpen it and make it work so that I have it for the rest of the day?" She didn't have anything else going on, so she agreed to come. I told her to just let me know when she got there and I'd come get her from the office. But then she arrived when we were leaving the library, so the kids saw her. You could just tell that they were confused. They asked, "Who's that?" and I said, "My husband," because I didn't know what to say. And you could tell that the wheels were kind of turning for some of them. It's just. . .**

Flint: It's complicated.

Mandy: **Yeah. It's bizarre and complicated.**

Flint: Because that's a situation that so many teachers find themselves in, right? Like, where you get this advice that feels so straightforward"Hey, don't share your life." You especially get that advice if you're queer. Like, don't share your life. But it's okay if you want to share pictures of your tortoise, right? But then they ask if your wife is your husband. And you have that moment where you have to either lie, and a little part of you, I'm sure, hurts—

Mandy: **Oh yeah**

Flint: Or you tell the truth then you end up in this moment of fear. Because the answer isn't actually, "Don't share your life." The answer is "this job will be easier if your life is different than the one that you have."

Mandy: You know, I just want to avoid the drama of it. Because I know that people are often stupid and ignorant, and getting people to evolve doesn't just happen, but sometimes you just have to in the moment be like, "Nope, not today. I'm not part of the solution today."

Flint: Not part of the solution today. I was just thinking about how often people call trans people "brave" for just waking up or existing, but sometimes I just want to wake up and just not be brave. I don't want to be brave today. I don't want to be a trailblazer. I just want to be alive; I want to be awake.

Mandy: The rock and a hard place feeling, right? Yeah, for sure.

Take a moment to journal through your thoughts regarding the story about Mandy's wife and the giant pencil. What feels challenging? Triggering? Frustrating? Familiar?

____

____

____

____

____

____

How should a colleague, administrator, school, or district support a teacher like Mandy who is facing a similar situation? How could she have been better supported at every level?

____

____

____

____

For a Birthday Girl

Before we finished our interview, Mandy asked if she could talk through an example from her time in the corporate world, when she worked for a major greeting card company.

Mandy: **So greeting cards are organized in stores in the way marketing people determine. Everything gets very granular, so in "kids' birthday," you have X amount of cards that are for boys and X amount of cards that are for girls. And then you have some that are just "kid." And after 20 years working for [company], we saw things changing.**

Flint: Changes in the birthday world.

Mandy: **Yeah, like why are we forcing "For a Super Cool Birthday Boy"? Why are we making this a boy card when you could keep it gender neutral and it would work for more people? You're limiting your market. But with the systems that we would have in place, there wasn't a way to change it. Trying to change these systems was like trying to redirect a cruise ship. Even though in theory, wouldn't it be better? You'd have to make fewer cards and you're opening your market up and you're making one card that can work twice as hard.**

Flint: That makes sense to me.

Mandy: **But then data would come back, and the cards that were bright pink and said "birthday girl" would sell better.**

Flint: Wait, really?

Mandy: **It's like with any corporation—you're following the money. So similarly, when you look into how to connect with people in moments of grief and loss, we know that platitudes and cliches aren't helpful, like "They're in a better place" and "Look on the bright side." That's not what people need and not what they want to hear. But you're not selling cards to the person receiving the cards; you're selling cards to the people who are buying them.**

So it doesn't really matter what the best thing is for the person receiving the card, you're having to do things for the person purchasing the card. And what the person purchasing the card might want is some really shitty platitudes. And so as

the creative team, you're fighting to make cards that are more inclusive and in line with what actually helps people, and you are having to defend it against financial results and metrics, which are often telling you something different.

So it's just kind of like a little snapshot into how often we get trapped into having to act against what we know is the best solution because people haven't caught up to us yet.

How does Mandy's experience in the world of greeting cards relate to what we're seeing with LGBTQ+ issues in the classroom?

____

____

____

____

____

____

Let's Recap:

What sticks out to you about Mandy's experiences? What are your overall reflections for this chapter?

____

____

____

____

What questions do you still have?

____

____

Teaching Like. . .I.C.

Pre-Quiz[8]

1. Which LGBTQ+ Civil Rights icon, elected to the San Francisco Board of Supervisors in 1977, was the first openly gay elected official in California?
   A. Alan Turing
   B. Harvey Milk
   C. Larry Kramer
   D. Thomas Lawrence Higgins
2. California was the birthplace of the gay pride rainbow flag in 1978. How many colors were featured in the flag's original design?
   A. 6
   B. 7
   C. 8
   D. 12
3. As of 2026, California is ranked as the state with the highest percentage of residents who speak Spanish at home.[9] What is that percentage?
   A. 10%
   B. 17.5%
   C. 22.1%
   D. 26.1%
4. The Fair, Accurate, Inclusive, and Respectful (FAIR) Education Act passed in California in 2011 mandates that social studies curricula in California public schools include the political, economic, and social contributions of LGBTQ+ figures throughout history. What other "underrepresented group" is included in the language of the FAIR Act?
   A. People with disabilities
   B. Black Americans
   C. Women
   D. Immigrants

[8] Answer Key: 1. B, 2. C, 3. D, 4. A.

[9] "Spanish Speaking States 2021." Worldpopulationreview.com, 2024, worldpopulationreview.com/state-rankings/spanish-speaking-states.

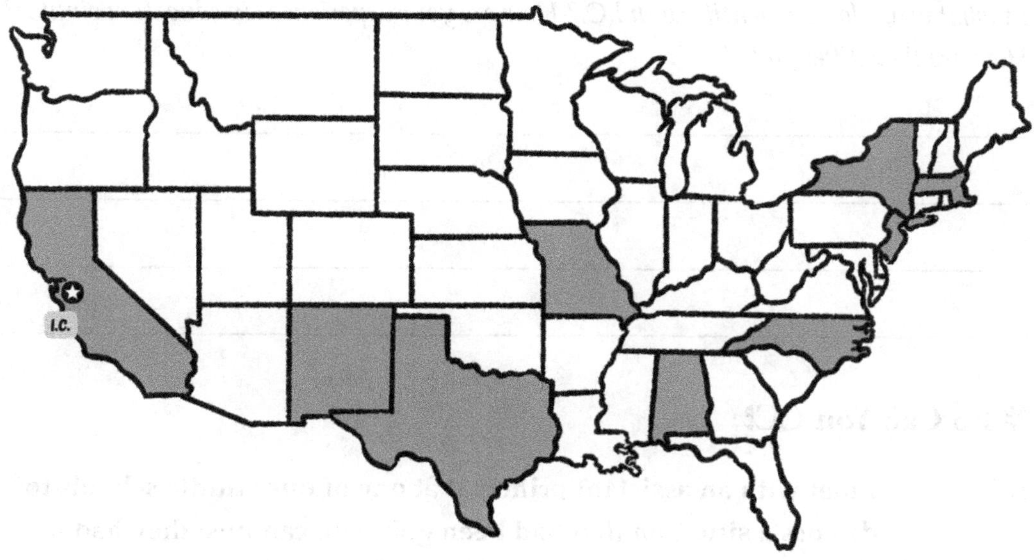

I.C. (he/him)
California
LGBTQ+ Counselor

When I.C.,[10] a school counselor who moved to the California Bay Area with his husband in the wake of the COVID-19 pandemic, learned that his school community was developing a district-wide LGBTQ+ counselor role, he jumped at the opportunity to serve the students who needed him most. "70 to 80% of my time is with students," he says, "with direct one-on-one services and support." With the rest of his time, I.C. shows up for the teachers and staff who serve in elementary and middle schools. "Part of my role in my district is providing professional development for schools," he says, "but I'm here for whoever needs me. Principals, counselors, teachers—everybody."

Based on your knowledge and/or assumptions about LGBTQ+ acceptance and protections in California, what are some of your worries, concerns, and hopes for I.C.'s experience?

____

____

____

____

[10] I.C. has chosen to go by his initials for anonymity.

In what ways do you identify with I.C.? How are your experiences in education similar? How are they different?

____

____

____

____

Who Can You CC?

I.C.: **I met with an assistant principal at one of our middle schools to discuss a situation that had been going on campus: they had a trans teacher who was being harassed by students.**

Flint: Alright wow, yeah. What's step 1 with something like that?

I.C.: **Well, you go through the matrix of discipline, right? So he brought me in to discuss—what more can we do? We want to support the teacher, obviously, but we also want these kids to understand what they're doing.**

Flint: And is this elementary? Middle school?

I.C.: **She teaches seventh and eighth grade.**

Flint: I would have loved it if someone like you had been called in when I was teaching. I think that would have been really helpful.

I.C.: **I think I found it challenging because I don't "do" discipline, and I don't know the matrix. So speaking to the AP, I asked, "Well, what have you done? Just kind of walk me through what you've already done."**

Flint: A good start.

I.C.: **And he said we've had a conversation with the counselors, the student, and the admin. And I asked, Have you brought the parents in? Have you tried a restorative conversation between the teacher and the student? We do have on campus a restorative justice TOSA[11] who focuses on having restorative conversations, and teachers really like to come to her. She helps support some of those challenging conversations, and so that was my suggestion.**

---

[11] TOSA stands for Teacher on Special Assignment and can designate a classroom teacher within a school district who takes on a specialized role either part- or full-time.

Flint: Love that.

I.C.: Right? Like let's share what we have already, and if I can be in those conversations, I'll do it gladly. Sometimes putting myself in that room to support the teacher is what I really need to do.

Flint: You just need someone in your corner. Teachers often don't have someone in their corner with them.

I.C.: I have a different example of that: one of my GSA advisors at an elementary school teaches fourth and fifth grade, and she doesn't feel like she has the support from her administrators. So she called me one day and said, If I send them an email, can I CC you? I was like, of course, CC me. For some reason, because I work in the district, people think I have some sort of power. I don't, right? But I will defend my queer staff or anyone who's supporting my queer students.

Flint: Hell yeah. You're ready in their corner.

I.C.: Exactly. Just having the support of someone else is important, who is also queer, who understands the nuances of being a queer individual in today's society, in the district, right? And so that's what I said. If I can be in that conversation with that restorative conversation with that teacher who's being harassed, and if you want to CC me on any emails, please do so.

Flint: Well, sometimes the power is even just having someone to CC at all, right?

I.C.: Yep.

Flint: When I was going through it in the classroom, I remember I was looking around like "Who's ready to show up?" and like "Who's gonna do anything about this?" Sometimes having anybody at all that's willing to be on that email? That's powerful.

I.C.: This happened last year too, when a school psychologist's email had gone back to their deadname, even though they had already switched it over to their preferred name. They immediately contacted me, we talked, and then we came up with a plan. I told her, let's email HR, and she asked, can I CC you? Absolutely. And there it was: the response was a lot different than when she originally tried to change her name. So I think you're right, Flint, I think just having anyone to CC matters. To be able to feel like, oh, there's someone else in my corner. It's very powerful. Yeah.

The role of a district-wide LGBTQ+ counselor is as rare as it is necessary. What do you think the scope of a role like this should be? What amount of responsibility and power is necessary to make this role effective? How do you know?

____

____

____

____

What does it mean to be "someone to CC"? How can you be this person for someone in your school community? Who could be this person for you?

____

____

____

____

Machisimo and Marianismo

I.C.: **The first student I started working with was pretty typical, I think, for middle school. He was ditching class, and teachers described him as having "difficult" or "challenging behavior."**

Flint: That sounds familiar, yeah.

I.C.: **Well, it turns out that he had been harassed in elementary school. He had been poked about his mannerisms and his tone of voice—"your gay lisp" as he said some kids would call it. He'd go into class and be called the f-slur and the teachers wouldn't say anything. So he started thinking, well if no one's gonna care about me at the school, why the eff am I here? Why am I trying? Why should I be in class when I'm being called an f-slur in the hallway? I worked with him for a year and a half and worked with his teachers. After a while, his behaviors diminished, and he's a lot more pleasant in class. His grades went up significantly too.**

Flint: Wow, that's great.

I.C.: **Working with his mom helped a lot. Sometimes parents just don't know how to support their kid, right? Because as Latinos, we don't talk about being queer. You'll hear, "Yes, I love my kid. I want to support him. I just don't know how." And mom didn't have the**

resources. I suggested that she ask her child if he feels like going to church with his family. Because in one of the conversations he shared that he had been prayed over—like to "pray the gay away."

Flint: Oh, wait—yikes.

I.C.: **Yes, right? We connected because he's also a Latino boy, you know, kind of figuring himself out in middle school and going to a house that's fairly religious at the same time, but with a mom that's supportive. Mom was trying to balance the religion and the support, but parents sometimes just have to hear, "Hey, your kid comes first." Let's focus on your kid and his well-being, and then you can adjust to it.**

Flint: It sounds like the role you serve in this is being able to connect not only with these individual students but also their families.

I.C.: **And the benefit of that is the culture, like the literal culture. My district is, I want to say, 80% or 75% Latiné, and in our culture, what we don't know, like anything queer, because of how our parents grew up, we kind of just try to put it aside. Within this culture of machismo and marianismo,[12] especially in Mexico, if you're queer, you're not a man. You have to be a man's man, right? Especially where [student's] family is from, Sonora, is more conservative—the rules are more defined. So when I'm speaking to his mom, I would always bring statistics in. I would share something like stats have shown that having one supportive person in their life can reduce [chance of self-harm or suicide] by such and such percent.[13] And I don't want to be that person. I love to be that person, but I would rather the mom or the dad or the parent be that person.**

Often "challenging behaviors" are a sign that something is happening under the surface with our students. How can we go about learning what that "something" could be? How are we limited from our positions, and who could we call on for help?

[12] Within Mexican culture, "machismo" can mean a sense of deeply-rooted masculinity based in dominance, aggression, and limited emotional expression. "Marianismo" is a similar cultural baseline for Latina femininity, often based in selflessness, nurturing, and submissiveness.

[13] The Trevor Project estimates that queer young people with at least one supportive adult in their life are 40% less likely to report a suicide attempt in the past year.

___

___

Here, I.C. dives into the cultural considerations that come up in his work within his district. What are some of the parallels between his community and yours?

___

___

What else would you want to share with the mother of this student? What resources or support might she still need?

___

___

I Am So Glad You're Here

I.C.: **I host a family event for the district, and the first year I had maybe 10 families show up. I did it again last year, and again I had probably the same 10 families. But there was one mom that showed up in the last 30 minutes by herself. And right at the end she started to share. She said, "My daughter's name is xyz, and I've noticed that she's started to act more masculine. I noticed at one of the soccer games that some of her friends were calling her 'him'." And this is one of those names that can really be either female or male.**

Flint: Like "Alex" or "Sam" or something.

I.C.: **Exactly. And she said that when they got home from the soccer game, she tried to ask about it, but her kid just immediately shut it down. They said they didn't want to talk about it. This mom was telling me, "I don't know what to do. I want to support my kid; I just don't know how."**

Flint: What a super brave thing to do, to show up to your event.

I.C.: **And in my head, I was thinking, "Oh, my God, I am so glad you're here. I am so glad that you're taking the time to ask questions." She and I sat down for like an hour and just talked one-on-one. I don't see enough parents showing up and asking the questions.**

Flint: That's wonderful. And do you remember? Do you remember what you said to her?

I.C.: **I remember sharing something that I had learned from a trans educator who led a workshop I attended. One example they shared was of a trans kid and their mother, where the kid shared that they wanted to start the process for top surgery. And even though mom was supportive, her response was "Can we first talk about it with a medical professional?" But what her kid heard was "no."**

What the trans educator was trying to tell us was that for trans individuals, they realize what they need from one day to the next—it can be that quick. So "hold on" can feel like a "no." Care with language is so important. So what I told the mom at the event was this: let the student lead, and just support wherever your kid is at.

Flint: Ah, yeah.

I.C.: **We—me and that mom—are not trans, right? We don't know the trans experience, and all we need to do is listen to what they're saying. If they change their mind three, four times? Let them change their mind three and four times. This is them exploring and figuring it out. Otherwise, we might make that movement stagnant by putting in our own biases or fears or anxieties. Go find support for that. There are support groups; there are parent support groups. But let's be on your kid's boat and just row behind them the whole time, whatever that looks like.**

In what ways can we "row behind a kid's boat" in our roles within a school community?

____

____

____

____

Use this space to list some questions you would like to ask the next time you're in an environment safe enough for vulnerable curiosity.

Four Corners

Flint: And you run trainings for teachers too, right?

I.C.: **Yes, and in those trainings, we've noticed that a lot of the teachers have a lot of anxiety around doing the "right things" or saying the right things or supporting students the "right way."**

Flint: There can be a lot of fear around this subject, that's for sure.

I.C.: **I always say, if you have good intentions, whatever you do is not going to eff up the kid. It's not going to harm them more, right? You asking, "Are you okay?" It's not going to harm this child.**

Flint: That's so true.

I.C.: **But, you know, the training is just to give them the tools. The specific training that I've done for these schools is how to stop harassment and bullying in the moment. Teachers tell me, "I just don't know what to say." But you can say, "Hey, stop. We don't use that language in my classroom." It can be that easy.**

Flint: We don't have to make this complicated.

I.C.: **The training is really just to help them dive into their own anxieties. One of the activities is, well, there are four corners, and every corner has a different response.**

Flint: I love four corners. I'm obsessed. I used this in my classroom all the time. Each corner is something like "Strongly Agree," "Agree, "Disagree. . .."

I.C.: **Yes, only for this we make them "I would speak to that person directly," "I would ignore it," "I would speak to the administrator," or "I would just walk away."**

Flint: Okay, wait, this is brilliant.

I.C.: **So an example is "You hear a colleague say something about a student being weak because he has two dads, and that's why he's being bullied," and then the teachers have to decide where they want to go. I'll often have somebody say, "I just feel really awkward standing here, because I wouldn't respond." But that's okay. It's an activity meant to help you realize where you're at. Maybe now it's easier to pull in a counselor or a social worker or your administrator when it actually happens. I think it's all just internal. Once you start speaking it out loud, you realize you do have other options.**

Flint: It's interesting to consider why so many educators are struggling to take a more active role in their school communities in moments like that.

I.C.: **I think right now honestly it's what they see on TV and the fears coming in from other states. You hear about teachers losing their jobs because of, you know, using a student's preferred name and pronouns, right? And so they have the same fears. Even in the training, I remind them, we live in California. We have the most protective factors for our students here in California. And the training? We align it with the California law. But they want to protect themselves. I get it. I was on the same boat at one point, too. But it's not getting us anywhere.**

Flint: Fear isn't a particularly effective educational strategy.

I.C.: **And the kids are just suffering. So listen to the kids. Speak to the kids. The kids know what they want. And then just honor what the kids want. If they say, "No one but you knows I want to be Alex and not Maria," then only I know. Okay then. I'll call them the name they want in this office, and then outside this office, it's back to Maria. We can do that for them.**

Flint: And again, the adults in your district—they have people they can call on, right? I'm thinking about how many people I'm talking to in parts of the country where they don't have these protective laws, where they are actively threatened. But in this case, you have educators that are in such a unique position where they're protected by California state law. They have someone they can CC. It's interesting that so many of them are still worried.

I.C.: **And it's usually the older, more seasoned teachers, if you will. I don't see the same anxiety, the same hesitation, in younger teachers who maybe just recently graduated, third, fourth, fifth year teaching; I'm talking about teachers who have been teaching for 10, 15, 20 years, who have a harder time with it.**

Flint: Yeah, it's hard to change. It's hard to do any kind of change.

How can we, as educators, administrators, and staff, manage the anxiety of this work in a way that leaves room for our LGBTQ+ students to thrive?

____

____

____

____

____

____

Let's Recap:

What sticks out to you about I.C.'s experiences? What are your overall reflections for this chapter?

____

____

____

____

What questions do you still have?

____

____

Teaching Like. . .Sean Em

Pre-Quiz[14]

1. Which of these terms means "to present with a feminine gender expression when assigned male at birth" though not necessarily strictly "as a woman"?
   A. Transmasc
   B. Trans woman
   C. Trans man
   D. Transfemme
2. Which of these terms can mean a gender identity that falls outside of the binary of "man" and "woman"?
   A. Nonbinary
   B. Genderqueer
   C. Pansexual
   D. All of these
   E. Just A and B

[14] Answer Key: 1. D, 2. E, 3. A, 4. C, 5. D.

3. Within the 2022 US Trans Survey,[15] the largest survey of trans Americans to date, what percentage of respondents self-identified as nonbinary?[16]

   A. 38%

   B. 35%

   C. 25%

   D. 2%

4. When broken down into gender identity by "gender assigned at birth," what percentage of US Trans Survey respondents self-identified as both nonbinary and assigned male at birth (AMAB)?

   A. 30%

   B. 25%

   C. 8%

   D. 2%

5. The Movement Advancement Project designates Massachusetts' pro-LGBTQ+ policy tally as "high." This puts them in the highest possible bracket for LGBTQ+ equality, sharing a designation with which other state featured in this workbook?

   A. North Carolina

   B. New Mexico

   C. Alabama

   D. New Jersey

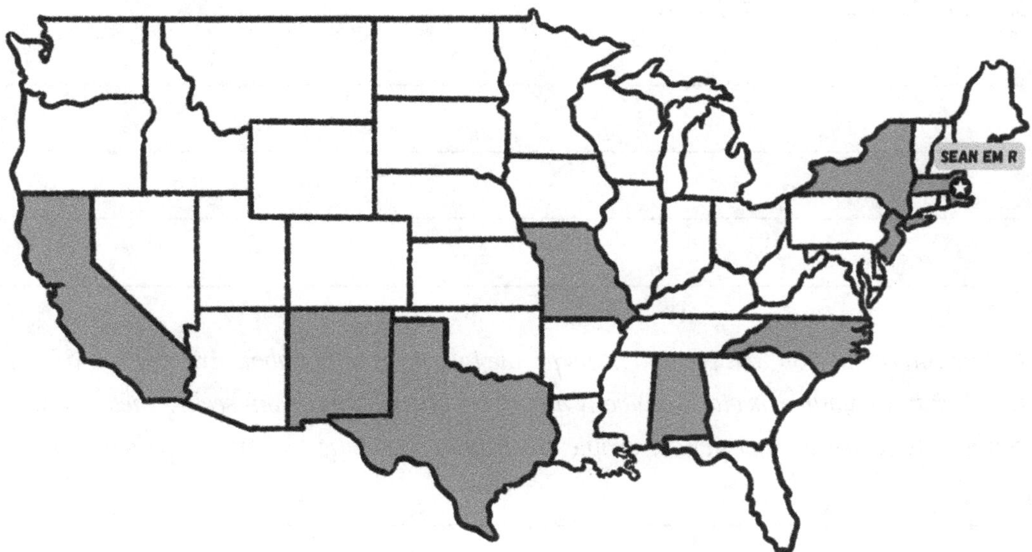

[15] "US Trans Survey." US Trans Survey, 2022, ustranssurvey.org/.

[16] The spelling of "nonbinary" is grammatically acceptable both with and without the hyphen. In the 2022 US Trans Survey, the organizers chose to use the variation without, as we do in this workbook.

Sean Em R (they/them)
Massachusetts
High School French Teacher

Though Sean Em—an autistic transfemme nonbinary public high school language teacher with a background in French sociophonetics and applied linguistics—has taught for more than a decade in a state with some of the most comprehensive protections for LGBTQ+ people in the United States, their experience within education still has room for growth when it comes to their relationship with their colleagues. "We can be so worried about upsetting allies that we don't lean into that bluntness when it's necessary," they say. "And it can get really exhausting."

Based on your knowledge and/or assumptions about LGBTQ+ acceptance and protections in Massachusetts, what are some of your worries, concerns, and hopes for Sean Em's experience?

____

____

____

____

In what ways do you identify with Sean Em? How are your experiences in education similar? How are they different?

____

____

____

____

In this interview, you will see two trans people talking together about trans life and identity. What are your expectations about how it will be different from seeing these kinds of conversations between cisgender people or between one trans and one cis person?

____

____

____

____

Calling In

[On "calling in"[17] a colleague who has made an error]:

Flint: So, how do we reach her? Like, how do we get to the person who wants to be there? You can tell [allies] often want to understand this stuff, but it can still feel so hard to confront them about it directly. Because we don't want to lose someone who could be on our side, but then they're not really on our side if they're not seeing us.

Seam Em: Sometimes I just take a very blunt tone. I say, "You say that you care about my well-being in this department, but it's been three years where you have been regularly misgendering me, so it seems like you need to do something and change your behavior."

Flint: And on the occasion they get it right, you can still sometimes see them, like, translating in their brain to the gender that you want to be seen as. I know that feeling so well. They don't actually *see* you. It's a really tough one to square.

Sean Em: And also it's just super unnecessary in most instances when you're talking to someone directly in front of you to talk about that person in the third person. It's pretty unnecessary. And you can avoid it, too. You can avoid gendering them completely.

Flint: Right?

Sean Em: I find myself in positions where a lot of cis people will describe me in the third person a little bit more often than I think they normally would with anyone else. It either consciously or subconsciously triggers their disconnect to how they see me, and then they "him" me or they "mister" me or they call me "Mr. R."

Flint: Hate that.

Sean Em: And I'm like, when have you seen me or have you ever talked to me once in this life where I am giving "Mr R"? Every single day—from day one with every colleague and all of my students—I go by "Sean." And if not, they call me "Prof" or "Professeur" or "Teacher." But really, everyone just calls me "Sean."

[17] "Calling in" (as opposed to "calling out") is the act of addressing biased or otherwise problematic behavior in a way that compassionately allows room for growth and repair.

What feelings are coming up as you read this exchange? Frustration? Familiarity? Defensiveness? Anger? Understanding?

____

____

If you are trans, how might you feel differently reading this as a trans ally? If you're an ally, how might it feel differently reading this as a trans person?

____

____

____

____

What do you consider to be the most effective strategy for "calling in" a potential ally? Why?

____

____

____

____

Social Capital and Social Currency

Sean Em: **I do have other queer colleagues in my department. When I do [directly "call in" problematic behavior], I usually get a pretty positive response from my boss, who is a younger Boomer cis woman. But when they [other queer colleagues] do that, they come more to blows with my department director.**

Flint: So, if they try to be more direct, they get a different response? What have you seen?

Sean Em: **I feel like it's [the administrator's] internalized sexism. I think that she inadvertently gives me more social capital and currency because she sees me as a man. It gives me a passive level of privilege. I have to face less scrutiny I think.**

Flint: You're hitting on something important. The same water that lifts the boat can also sink it, right? There are privileges that you are being afforded specifically because someone is not seeing you. And that's not good. Like, that's not a good thing. Nothing is solved with that.

Sean Em: And I lose out on that, too. Because if a person looks at me as a man and misgenders me and invalidates my gender identity, they still want me to take it as a compliment that they're not actively harassing me or calling me a [slur] or pushing me out of the workplace. Yes, you're not actively causing me immense personal harm. That's great. I appreciate that. But that's the bare minimum. I shouldn't have to beg for more.

Sean Em theorizes that they and their other queer colleagues are the subject of internalized misogyny. How else does misogyny show up in education spaces?

____

____

____

____

Make a comparison chart here. On one side, list behaviors and accommodations that we might consider the "bare minimum" in a school workplace for a trans teacher. On the other, list others that challenge us to ask for "more" in our fight for workplace equity.

Psychological Safety

Sean Em: **I have a certain level of psychological comfort and safety in my job, but there's obviously some smallish but still ever-present noticeable amount of a lack of certainty around how safe I am to be my fullest truest self. It affects me more than I think I usually let on with people.**

Flint: I think that phrase, the idea of "psychological safety," is one that we don't talk about enough. We are a little bit in our "crumbs" era as trans people right now. Just not being fired for being trans is such a gift in so many places.

Sean Em: **I'll never be sure that a person is actually looking at me as a nonbinary person or if they believe me or if they're just saying they do because they know that it would cause them more social friction to actively misgender me. Because really I don't care about pronouns; I care about "Do you see me as a transgender person?" and "Do you believe me when I tell you who I am?"**

It's a continual back-and-forth or like a tug-of-war between fighting the "good fight" and experiencing constant micro-oppression all the time. It's a challenge that I appreciate, but I would be lying to you, Flint, if I said that since COVID especially, it hasn't weighed on me in a kind of harsher, deeper, different way. It weighs on a different part of my heart than it used to.

Flint: I'm sure. Because it might seem small, but it's like you have this slow dripping water torture you're dealing with over the course of years, where you're like, yes, I'm here, but also it's slowly eroding a sense of self that you deserve to have when you're at work.

What does "psychological safety" mean to you?

____

____

____

____

Sean Em describes the "micro-oppression" of working as a nonbinary teacher. What do you think that means? What are some other examples of "micro-oppressions"?

____

Let's Recap:

What sticks out to you about Sean Em's experiences? What are your overall reflections for this chapter?

What questions do you still have?

Teaching Like. . .Stanley

Pre-Quiz[18]

1. According to the Math Learning and Identity Project,[19] a survey that collected responses from more than 90,000 high school students, what percentage of respondents agreed with the statement "It is important for everyone to learn math"?
   A. 46%
   B. 57%
   C. 61%
   D. 70%

[18] Answer Key: 1. B, 2. A, 3. D, 4. D.

[19] "Making Sense of Learning Math: Insights from the Student Experience – YouthTruth Survey." YouthTruth Survey, 10 Apr 2025, youthtruth.org/resources/making-sense-of-learning-math-insights-from-the-student-experience/.

2. According to the 2022 US Trans Survey,[20] what percentage of respondents reported holding a graduate degree or higher?
   A. 7%
   B. 15%
   C. 19%
   D. 24%
3. In what year did North Carolina pass House Bill 805, defining sex as a permanent and immutable category, and implying that transgender people's gender identity would never be legally recognized under state law?
   A. 1920
   B. 1965
   C. 1999
   D. 2025
4. Which of these laws are, as of 2026, currently active in North Carolina?
   A. A "Don't Say Gay" law, restricting educators from discussing LGBTQ+ people or issues in K12 classrooms
   B. A law preventing transgender students from participating in a sport consistent with their gender identity
   C. A law requiring "forced outing" of transgender student to their parent or guardian before school staff can use a student's preferred name or pronouns
   D. All of the above

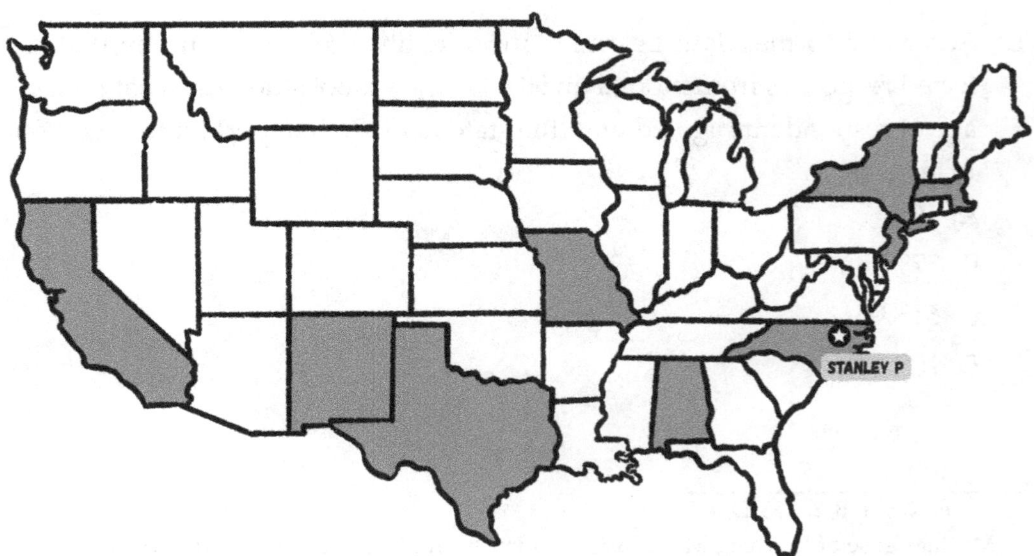

[20] "US Trans Survey." US Trans Survey, 2022, ustranssurvey.org/.

Stanley P (he/him)
North Carolina
College Adjunct Mathematics Instructor

Stanley, a mathematics graduate student, adjunct instructor, and mixed-race Southeast Asian transgender man, has lived and worked in the world of collegiate academia for the entirety of his adult life. "I've gotten to teach at a large public university, a private PWI,[21] a HBCU,[22] and now a two-year college," he says, "and there's a relationship between poor pedagogy, widespread math anxiety, and minoritized students feeling like they don't belong in math spaces." As a queer math instructor, Stanley's position is clear: "I am a firm believer that anyone can learn mathematics with the right support."

Based on your knowledge and/or assumptions about LGBTQ+ acceptance and protections in North Carolina, what are some of your worries, concerns, and hopes for Stanley's experience?

___

___

___

___

In what ways do you identify with Stanley? How are your experiences in education similar? How are they different?

___

___

___

___

[21] A PWI is a "Predominantly White Institution," meaning a higher education institution where white students make up a majority of the enrolled population.
[22] Historically Black Colleges and Universities.

Will the Queer Mathematicians in the Room Please Stand Up

Stanley: **One really big issue that I've run into a lot is that there are just so few queer people in math spaces. You know, there is a national organization for queer mathematicians, and I'm part of that—**

Flint: Wait, I know. . .hold on. I know the answer to this. You're in the middle of a sentence, and I don't want to interrupt you, but I also am really excited that I might have put this in my. . .[thumbs through *Teach Like an Ally*] Classroom Policies, Physical Environment, Units and Lessons. Okay. By Subject. . .Math. . .Is it Spectra?

Stanley: **It is Spectra.**

Flint: Incredible! It's listed right here. I have LGBTQ issues in math—Spectra. And then I talk about people like Alan Turing, right? And Sophie Wilson. Anyway, I'm so excited that that's something you're a part of. What do you do in that organization?

Stanley: **Well, I would love it if there were enough queer mathematicians that we could have a departmental club or something, you know? In theory, that is something Spectra does, but I'm unsure how many institutional chapters there actually are. There are so few queer mathematicians and, often, I think if there are no queer mathematicians in the room and people are making a decision involving including queer students, that decision is almost always going to be the wrong decision.**

Flint: Now that sounds familiar.

Stanley: **It just amazes me how bad the perspectives can be when you don't have a queer person there to state the obvious. That lack of representation, combined with the lack of knowledge from nonqueer mathematicians—it's quite bad. There's a real need for more education on how to be a better ally and how to teach inclusively.**

Flint: I'm fully in the English world, right? You can throw a stick in any room full of English teachers and hit a gay one. We're just everywhere. What are some of the issues you think you need more queer voices in the room for? What tends to come up? What's top of mind for you?

Stanley: **One issue is that most mathematicians don't know what the issues are.**

Flint: Well, there you go.

Stanley: **Mathematics as a field definitely struggles with diverse representation. When you look at mathematics faculty, it is a very old, male, cishet, white, upper class—**

Flint: I have the image, yeah.

Stanley: **So even identifying what issues there are, culturally, within math. . .a lot of people, specifically faculty, have trouble even identifying what's wrong, because they haven't experienced it personally.**

Stanley mentions that without queer representation in mathematics spaces, "most mathematicians don't know what the issues are." Where do you see similar issues in your own school community? Whose perspective is missing? What is lost without it?

____

____

____

____

Nothing Gay About Differential Equations

Stanley: **Something else we struggle with is this: how do we talk about queer identities in math spaces? In other fields, like English or psychology, there's sort of a natural reason to be discussing identity, but mathematicians really like to think of math as a super "objective" thing, right? Like, we're going to come in here, and we're going to solve differential equations. There's nothing gay about differential equations!**

Flint: You would think!

Stanley: **A lot of mathematicians really don't want to "make things political" because it doesn't seem relevant, but secretly it is relevant. It does come up.**

Flint: Where do you see it?

Stanley: **With queer students, there are usually very few of them. We struggle a lot with positive representation of queer stories in math. When we talk about mathematicians and their work, we don't usually talk a lot about biography or history. So students often don't recognize that there are actual people behind the math they're doing.**

Flint: I don't remember ever learning much about them.

Stanley: Exactly! Someone discovered that thing that we're using, and you could discover something too. Do you know how to create your own math? And if there is a little biography sketch in the textbook, it usually won't mention their identity or the larger context in which they were coming up with this stuff. And so maybe students have seen queer mathematicians, but the book just didn't mention that they were queer if it talked about this person on a personal level at all.

Flint: Yeah.

Stanley: And there are so many other ways in which math is pretty political, and that can send a message to queer students as well. If faculty are saying "I don't want to make things political" when it comes to talking about [queerness] in math spaces but then they're advertising all these defense scholarships and telling their students to apply to work in surveillance? That's political. That sends a message.

Whose lives and identities do we consider "political" in the classroom? Whose do we not?

____

____

____

____

Consider your position and content area within education. Do you find it more or less "natural" to discuss LGBTQ+ issues, or is there a perceived barrier? Why or why not?

____

____

____

____

The Textbook on the Table

Stanley: **So, most courses are going to have a course textbook, and for the most part those courses will follow the textbook pretty closely, especially if it's an upper-level course. Something interesting about these textbooks is that they're very far behind in how they portray people.**

Flint: How so?

Stanley: **Well, first, as we talked about already, there's a lot of history missing. People don't produce math in a bubble, and it's nice to know facts like "These guys were friends, and that's why they like came up with a lot of similar stuff, because they were riffing off of each other" or "During this period of time, this was how people thought about math" or "This person was queer, and they dealt with a lot of oppression, so that's why they didn't make as much progress in their research and why we have these unanswered questions."**

Flint: That kind of context can really help when you're engaging with something that doesn't feel super friendly to students who are already struggling with it.

Stanley: **Yes, and you'll sometimes have these much older textbooks where they're like typeset using a typewriter, and all of the math symbols are handwritten in pen. It's almost impossible to read because the language is so old.**

Flint: Hard pass.

Stanley: **But also there's this larger issue of how they perpetuate stereotypes about gender.**

Flint: Wait, what?

Stanley: **For example, if we look at pretty much any textbook that's more than 40 years old, they will always address the reader as "he."**

Flint: Not a great starting point.

Stanley: **Things have improved a little bit. Now, most textbooks will use "he or she," but I would love to see the singular "they."**

Flint: And hey, we've been using "they" as a third person singular pronoun since pre-Shakespeare. So yeah.

Stanley: **It's also been really interesting to see this in how exercises are written. This happens more in earlier math courses, your "gen ed" type courses, where it would be plausible to have a person in the problem. Because, you know, in a more theoretical context, the example problem is just going to be. . .**

Flint The textbooks that I'm reading in high school and college are the ones that have people in them.

Stanley: **Right, where they'll have these problems where Mary has 100 watermelons or whatever. It's really fascinating reading those examples, because, one, you'll notice that they will often enforce the standard of whiteness. All of the names that they pick are very Western-sounding names. And they really enforce gender stereotypes in a lot of ways, because if you look at these example problems, it's always "Mary is baking cookies and Bob is playing basketball" or something like that.**

Flint Mary isn't working on the space shuttle.

Stanley: **Right, exactly. It enforces power structures with how we talk about gender, because Mary is baking cookies or Mary is measuring things for a quilt, but then Bob owns companies, Bob is buying stock, Bob is getting a promotion.**

Flint Bob isn't changing a diaper.

Stanley: **Nope. So you get these very ambitious scenarios from masculine-sounding characters. There are actually a lot of opportunities for positive representation in math, which I think a lot of people don't see. I was having a discussion a while back about representation for people with disabilities in math spaces. Like what about ADA specifications, right? Designing ramps that are up to code? There's trigonometry in there. There's stuff about slope in there, and that's actually a real world use, and it acknowledges that disabled people exist. So what if math textbooks were more like that?**

Flint I love that. Really, what you're saying is opening up math spaces to every kind of representation that allows students to feel seen in the world that they exist in.

Imagine you are designing a math problem asking students to solve the following equation: $4x - 2 = 14$. How might you write a word problem that avoids the pitfalls of many older math textbooks?

Alternate Option: *If you broke out into hives at the sight of algebra, you're welcome to try this with some simpler math. How about 100 – 50 = ?*

____

____

____

____

____

____

We shape our students' perception of the world with not only our own language and actions but by the art, texts, and resources they see in our classrooms every day. Where do you see this in your own educational experiences?

____

____

____

____

Deadnamed by the Printer

Stanley: **A prior graduate program of mine had something like 60 students. I'd often be the only trans person, or maybe one of two. There were always very few queer people in these spaces, and there's a lot of intersection between being trans and other identities, right?**

Flint: That's common, yeah.

Stanley: **I grew up solidly middle class, maybe lower middle class, with a single mom. You don't see that in those spaces. And when it comes to talking about things like neurodiversity—these are identities we don't see a lot. Being underrepresented in some way was tough, and it continues to be tough. These spaces select for a particular type of person, and if you're able to get to a point where you have a successful career in research, you probably have some type of privilege.**

Flint: I can imagine.

Stanley: **It was interesting to see how the logistics of being a trans person played out. The name change process was such a pain. Mathematicians really struggle to understand how having some sort of marginalized identity actually affects you. Like, genuinely, queer folks have fewer hours in the day. When I was doing my name change, I found out the hard way that a university is a very decentralized place. There's no one person that you contact and say, "I've changed my name; what do I do?" You talk to the registrar, you talk to the tech people—there's just no centralized advice on who to contact. It took months. I would be on the phone with people probably at least once a week working on my name change. And just when you think that you fixed everything, like two semesters later you'd get deadnamed by one specific campus printer.**

Flint: Getting deadnamed by a printer is a special kind of middle finger.

Stanley: **It is, yeah.**

What do you think Stanley means when he says, "Queer folks have fewer hours in the day"?

____

____

____

____

What are some of the potential academic and social consequences a trans person might face from being deadnamed, both as a student and as an instructor?

____

____

____

____

Teachers in the Basement

Stanley: **Before we wrap up, I should mention that in math, a lot of women and queer folks are pigeonholed into teaching positions.**

Flint: That's an interesting one. Why do you think that is?

Stanley: **I don't know how it is in other fields, so I'm not going to speak for them, but in mathematics, they really de-emphasize teaching. The cultural expectation of what I was taught throughout my education, when I knew I wanted to be a professor, was that spending time on pedagogy was a waste of time. Your goal, they told me, is to do your research. The more time you spend on teaching, the less time you have to spend on research.**

Flint: So it's about prioritizing your time?

Stanley: **Yes, you want to spend as little time and effort on teaching as possible. And I experienced that firsthand. When I started grad school, the pedagogy was awful. As mathematicians, none of us has formal training. No one has a degree or has even taken a course in education. You never receive any sort of training or discussion around teaching or mentoring students—it's just something you get thrown into one day. It's just an obligation that you have to do, like checking emails. It's not something you want to get better at. And because of that, teaching is hugely devalued. At my previous institution, there were the "Faculty" faculty who had tenure and certain protections and nice offices, and then there were "teaching" faculty who were hired under a different title like "lecturer," and they didn't have the protections that tenure comes with. They were almost exclusively women and queer people, and their offices were in the basement.**

Flint: Wow—way to get super literal about it.

Stanley: **Yeah. And so it's just fascinating to see, because all of those people who spend time on teaching and care about students as people also have these identities themselves. They're the ones who are showing up to be on a DEI committee or the "student outcomes" committee. They're putting in all this work, and they're the ones who are getting talked over when the committee talks to the department chair or the dean. They don't get listened to or taken seriously or followed up on.**

Flint The devaluing of women and queer folks always seems to go hand in hand. So many of these groups are getting away with this for so long because they have these small DEI groups they don't end up actually taking advice from.

Stanley: **Yep. You end up just on the same carousel over and over again.**

What might a "de-emphasis" of teaching and pedagogy communicate to university students who are studying mathematics?

___

___

___

___

What groups of educators, staff, and community members show up to subgroups and committees in your school community? Whose voices are missing? Why?

___

___

___

___

Lesson Idea[23]

How can we share more diverse and complete narratives with students of mathematics?

Investigate mathematical objects, theories, and principles with your students, and ask what stories their names tell us about both the people who discovered them and the societies who still use them today.

[23] Lesson idea and examples courtesy of Stanley P.

Examples:

- Sombrero Potential
- Hawaiian Earring
- Sudanese Möbius strip (*named for creators Sue Goodman and Daniel Asimov, not for the nation of Sudan*)

Who is named, and who is unnamed, in our study of mathematics?

Examples:

- Euler's Formula (named for discoverer Leonhard Euler)
- Taylor's Theorem (named for discoverer Brook Taylor)
- Chinese Remainder Theorem

Let's Recap:

What sticks out to you about Stanley's experiences? What are your overall reflections for this chapter?

____

____

____

____

What questions do you still have?

____

____

Teaching Like. . .Matthew

Pre-Quiz[24]

1. Texas Senate Bill 8 (the "Women's Privacy Act") bans transgender people from using restrooms consistent with their gender in all K-12 schools, colleges, and government-owned buildings. What is the civil penalty for any state agency found in violation of this policy?
   A. $500 for a first offense, $1,000 for the second
   B. $1,500 for a first offense, $10,000 for the second
   C. $15,000 for a first offense, $25,000 for the second
   D. $25,000 for a first offense, $125,000 for the second
2. In what year did the Manhattan Club, Austin's first gay bar, open?
   A. 1906
   B. 1922
   C. 1958
   D. 1973
3. Which 2003 Supreme Court case ruled that Texas's "Homosexual Conduct" law violated the fourteenth amendment, effectively decriminalizing consensual same-sex sexual activity across the United States?
   A. Milk v. Texas
   B. Del Sol v. Texas
   C. Palomino v. Texas
   D. Lawrence v. Texas
4. In the 2025 legislative session, Texas lawmakers filed more than 200 anti-LGBTQ+ bills,[25] more than any other state in the history of the country. How many of these were passed by the Legislature and sent to Governor Greg Abbott's desk to be signed into law?
   A. 12
   B. 100
   C. 20
   D. 6

[24] Answer Key: 1. D, 2. C, 3. D, 4. A.

[25] DiPaolo, Joelle. "Here Are the New Anti-LGBTQ Bills Texas Passed into Law." The Texas Observer, 4 June 2025, www.texasobserver.org/texas-lege-2025-anti-lgbtq-bills-passed/.

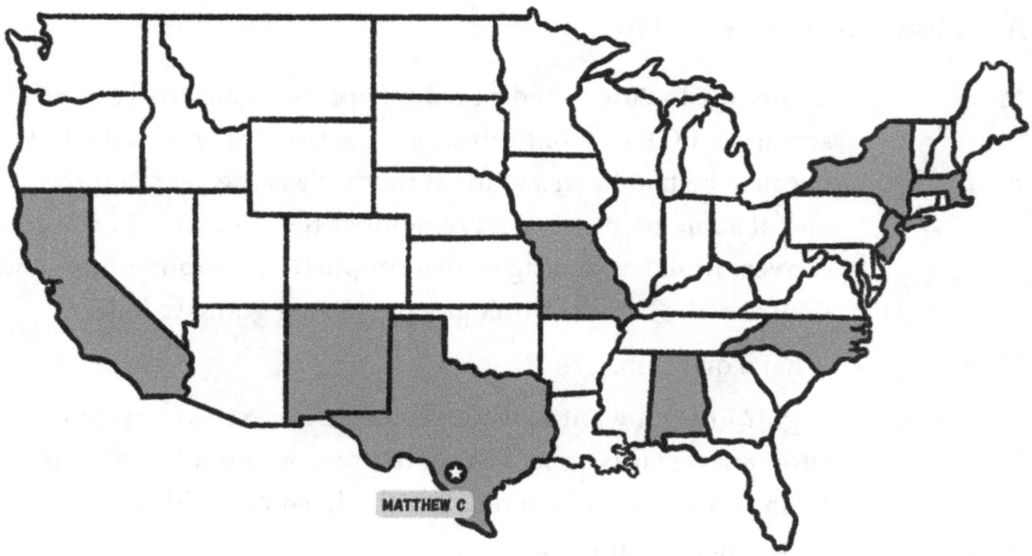

Matthew C (he/him)
Texas
High School Social Studies and Journalism Teacher

Matthew has been teaching at a low-income high school in the same South Texas town for 16 years, and he says that in his time in the classroom, his commitment to his home has only gotten stronger, even though he has plenty of criticisms about the way his state sees the value of his students. "The area where I can leverage my privilege," he says, "is within the confines of my classroom."

Based on your knowledge and/or assumptions about LGBTQ+ acceptance and protections in Texas, what are some of your worries, concerns, and hopes for Matthew's experience?

____

____

____

____

In what ways do you identify with Matthew? How are your experiences in education similar? How are they different?

____

____

____

____

My Short Answer Was "No"

Matthew: **Sometime in 2014, I had a student approach me about sponsoring an LGBT club. I think that the student approached me because he had been a student in my class the year before, and at some point—I don't remember the context—there's a conversation happening with a couple of my sophomores, and they asked, "Do you think gay people are going to hell?"**

Flint What a question.

Matthew: **Right? I didn't want to weigh too much into theology, but my short answer was "no." I think that was enough to signal to them "Okay, he's like a reliable ally in some fashion."**

Flint I'd call that a solid minimum, yeah.

Matthew: **And this is pre-Obergefell,[26] but not by much. At any rate, now I run this "not-technically-GSA-but-wink-wink-if-you-know-you-know" kind of club. I officially ran the club from 2014 to 2025, when Senate Bill 12 passed in the Texas legislature. Effective September 1 after that, that club could not exist explicitly as an LGBT-affirming place, so we rebranded.**

Flint: What were you calling the club before?

Matthew: **Sexuality and Gender Awareness, the "SGA."**

Flint: And now?

Matthew: **We're called "CUSS": Clearly United for School Service.[27]**

Flint: Okay, that's adorable.

Matthew: **But the main purpose of the club is mostly social, more than anything. We've had students for whom activism is an important part of what they do and what they wanted from the club, so that was kind of like what they pushed for.**

Flint: What did that look like?

Matthew: **Early on in the club experience, I had some students initiate the National Day of Silence, and I taught that day in complete silence, which was an interesting experiment. I wrote things down on legal pads a lot.**

---

[26] Obergefell v. Hodges is the 2015 Supreme Court decision ruling that the fundamental right to marry extended to same-sex couples within the United States.

[27] Club name has been modified for anonymity.

Flint: That sounds complicated, but what a cool moment of solidarity with your students.

Matthew: It was, yeah. I kind of had to create assignments that could be done, more or less, self-directed. But, you know, we made it work that day.

Flint: Incredible.

Matthew: That same year, I had students who wanted to go before the school board and talk about bathroom access, so we went and spoke before the board that day.

Flint: That's a really great "starter" activist activity for those super-motivated GSA students.

Matthew: Yeah. And when that group of students graduated, the next group was not as political, I would say. They just wanted a place to hang out with friends and feel kind of normal, you know?

Flint: Yeah. I feel like that's a pendulum you can experience when you run GSAs for any extended period of time.

Matthew: So, that's just kind of what it became. We have after-school game sessions, we plan little activities, that kind of thing. In many respects—and maybe this sounds weird—it functions more or less like a church youth group in some ways, without the proselytizing. It's just like all the sort of ancillary social things that you would get from a youth group. That's kind of what it was. It was a youth group, but just, instead of doing a prayer candle, we answer some weird question of the day and tell us your pronouns if you want to.

According to the ACLU,[28] Texas's SB12 ***"bars all programs and activities that mention race, ethnicity, gender identity, or sexual orientation in K-12 public schools in Texas,"*** *and also bans* ***"Gender and Sexuality Alliances (GSAs), inhibits teachers' ability to support transgender students, and stops students from receiving information about gender identity or sexual orientation in every grade level from kindergarten through 12th grade."***

[28] "ACLU of Texas, SEAT Will Sue over S.B. 12—Texas Law That Prohibits Programs and Discussions Involving Race, Gender Identity, and Sexual Orientation in K-12 Schools - ACLU of Texas." ACLU of Texas, 15 Dec 2025, www.aclutx.org/press-releases/aclu-texas-seat-will-sue-over-sb-12-texas-law-prohibits-programs-and-discussions/.

What were Matthew's other options after the passing of SB12, and why do you think he didn't choose to explore them? What would you have done in his place?

____

____

____

____

What are some reasons why a group of students within a GSA might pivot from an "activist" role to a more "social" one?

____

____

____

____

In the Name of Parental Rights

Flint: What, specifically, does SB12 ban? What had to change for you?

Matthew: It's pretty wide-sweeping, and a lot of this is done in the name of "parental rights." I think there's this effort on the part of the state to cut off as many support structures as possible for queer kids. It's like "We want to make sure that no professional adult around you is ever going to say that it's okay to be who you are. We need to make sure that only your parents get to decide what's okay for you and what's not." It is now illegal, for example, for school staff to refer to a child by any name other than the one on their birth certificate, and that can be sanctioned through not only losing your job but also potentially losing your license.

Flint: That's truly bonkers.

Matthew: I think they realize that a lot of the stuff they want to do is unenforceable. What they really want is to have snitches on the inside. They want to have like the surveillance state in schools, which is pretty limited because you can't set up cameras inside classrooms yet.

Flint: Not yet!

Matthew: **No, not yet. So they need some of the type of people who are just going to snoop in and say, "I heard this teacher using this pronoun with this kid and then ratting them out."At any rate, SB12 is part of a broader legislative assault on queer kids in general. I'm part of PFLAG,[29] and a lot of people [within Texas] join because PFLAG is engaged in a lawsuit against the state, so if you are a PFLAG member, you gain some degree of legal protection because you're part of a plaintiff group, and that way you can continue to be a good parent to your trans kids and not suffer the slings and arrows of the state.**

Flint: I can imagine being the parent of a trans child in Texas is incredibly difficult right now.

Matthew: **There are many parents in our group who have already left Texas or have left the country entirely. Many of the parents who are in the group who have adult-aged children experienced a much easier time raising a trans kid 10 years ago than they do now, because trans kids weren't yet this political hot-button issue. Ten years ago, it was barely on anybody's radar, and now the concentration of right-wing media attacks has made trans kids their main focus in a lot of respects, because it's easy "culture war" points to make ignorant and bigoted people scared.**

Flint: It's a pretty classic move, politically.

Matthew: **You can distract them with this "threat" of trans kids while like their other quality-of-life issues just kind of continue to go down the crapper. We could be updating our power grid or focusing on housing affordability. There are a lot of issues in Texas that they're just never going to address because they can continue to scavenge enough votes off of fear-mongering.**

Many of Matthew's perspectives regarding allied teaching are rooted in the politics of his home state. In what way, if any, do educators have an obligation to understand and participate in the political world?

____

____

[29] PFLAG is an LGBTQ+ advocacy organization whose name was originally an acronym standing for "Parents and Friends of Lesbians and Gays."

___

___

The issues that we consider "political" are constantly changing, as Matthew illustrates with experiences with the parents of trans children. Whose lives do we consider "political" and whose do we not? Why?

___

___

___

___

A Culture of Distrust

Flint: Does all of this, from your perspective, create any kind of culture of distrust in your school community?

Matthew: **Really, if you have a school full of supportive people who are in disagreement with a particular law, who's going to make them comply?**

Flint: That's a good point.

Matthew: **It's not even just who has the authority but who has the desire to enforce it, right? If you have an anti-gay or anti-trans law on the books and you have gay and trans people working in your school and you have enough supportive allies in place. . .even if you have people who disagree or are unapproving or have some bigoted views, they might not want to rock the boat socially, because they become potentially outcast in their social circle. That creates an environment where it's like—who's going to enforce this? Who's going to actually do it? Somebody has to be like "Everybody in here is being super supportive, and I can't stand it!"**

Flint: [laughs]

Matthew: **Right? "I have to step in! Somebody has to step in and stop all of this. . .gentleness! Somebody has to be punished!" There has to be somebody there who, through a crisis of conscience or something, believes that some real harm is being done. And that that could sometimes be because they have personal**

beef with the person, you know? I have to be—kind of—on my "best behavior" in some ways and not piss off certain people, because what if they say, "Well, I totally know how I could get [Matthew] now, because I can just dial up my local state agent," and then that's all it takes. They can start an investigation. It doesn't even have to be somebody who goes to that school—it can be a parent, a teacher, a student. Anybody who has eyes on the situation and knows that this power exists is now authorized through this bill to snitch.

Flint: Wow.

Matthew: Yeah, that's all they really have to do to make this work.

What effect does a "culture of distrust" have on members of a school community other than teachers? What might the effect be on students? Families? Administrators? Other school staff?

____

____

____

____

____

____

Matthew: I look at this job as part of a broader commitment to justice.

Flint: Okay, wait, say more about that.

Matthew: I am a non-Latino white person, and I've grown up in [South Texas] my whole life, but I grew up on the north side, which is where the white people of [South Texas town] live due to our history of spatial geographic segregation. The west side, where I teach, has been predominantly Latino for the last 100 years. It started off, essentially, as a refugee camp during the Mexican revolution, and it was on the outskirts of town. It was not a desirable area, it was very flood prone, and the city did not invest in infrastructure there. It was a shanty town for decades and it was even the site of a major tuberculosis outbreak in the 30s.

Flint: Wow.

Matthew: So here I am from the north side, and there's that sort of stereotypical white savior, like, "I'm going to show these kids how to get educated." But I didn't have a clue. I didn't have the cultural toolkit, right, to connect with people who did not share my upbringing and didn't share my privileges.

Flint: Yeah, like you're not about to swoop in and solve 100 years or more of structural racism.

Matthew: Exactly. Most of my kids who are going to college are first-generation college students. They are scraping together essays and scholarship applications, trying to get financial aid packages, and that's just for the kids who are going. For a good number of our students, they're going to go straight into the workforce or the military. It's just a different set of expectations, a different set of cultural norms. The school system, in other words, was designed for people like me to succeed.

Flint: And there's sometimes a different definition of what "success" means.

Matthew: Failure, it's built into the system. The amount of inequality that our school system creates—it's designed. Consider this: how do you know that your kid goes to a good school district? You need to have bad school districts to compare them to. So, if we systematically deprive these people of resources, both in and outside of the school system, they're going to perform worse. And that way, you know you got the good deal, right? That's part of the social contract of inequality: enough people have to buy into it because, "hey, my kids got theirs."

Flint: There are a lot of teachers who don't ask a lot of questions about their school population, who are content not to think too hard about it.

Matthew: I think you have to, if you work in a low-income school district. If you come in with this belief of superiority or trust in the hierarchy, you're never going to respect your kids. You're never going to try to understand them on a deeper, more personal level. You're always going to appear judgmental. Kids can detect when you're not being real with them.

Flint They absolutely can.

Matthew: **People who retain those beliefs really struggle to connect with their kids, and they don't typically last. They don't last very long because they find the job too stressful. They don't realize the extent to which they are bringing their baggage into this job, and they just blame the kids. They're like, "These kids can't behave." And they can. It's hard sometimes for them to regulate their emotions, but if you have basic respect for them and a relentless respect for their intellectual gifts and possibilities, they'll rise to the level you treat them.**

Part of Matthew's connection with his students comes from an understanding of their context and the history of their community. Take a moment to reflect on similar knowledge you have about the history and context of your own school community. What do you think you still have to learn?

____

____

____

____

What do you think Matthew meant by "a relentless respect for their intellectual gifts and possibilities"? What does this look like in the classroom and within a school community as a whole?

____

____

____

____

The Default American

Matthew: **In large part, the privilege that I bring into the job is, for a lot of people, I'm their idea of the "default" American. I am able, I think, to get away with more because I don't have a lot of targets on my back because of my identity.**

Flint: Because you're bringing in more of what you might consider "radical" texts into your social studies classroom, right? You're reading Char Miller's *West Side Rising* and assigning podcasts from one of the authors of *Forget the Alamo* and whatnot.

Matthew: I think it's easier for me to do that as a white person, right? As a white person, some people assume you have the "neutral" position, which is silly, right? That's obviously false. But, I think that makes it easier to introduce these kinds of texts.

Flint: Yeah, you're considered "ideologically neutral." When we think about the "default person," that's not a real thing.

Matthew: That's not a thing. But when you can operate from a place where people feel that's where you're coming from, yeah.

Flint: I'm having this moment right now where I'm realizing I started transitioning about halfway through my teaching career. So, for a long time, I was a "nice white lady" who got away with a lot. Then the second I started to realize that I was queer and started transitioning, all of a sudden the things that I was already teaching became political, became something that was being used to "further an agenda." They started thinking of me less as a neutral presence.

Matthew: Yeah, it's like your identity is now legible to people as a threat. It's fascinating.

Is classroom "neutrality" achievable, possible, or real? Why or why not?

____

____

____

____

____

____

Let's Recap:

What sticks out to you about Matthew's experiences? What are your overall reflections for this chapter?

____

____

____

____

What questions do you still have?

____

____

GSA Calendar Map

If you're the advisor for a campus GSA like Matthew, you might be familiar with the challenges of developing any kind of consistent structure for the students you're hosting from week to week. One way to construct a sense of purpose and maintain low-stakes expectations (for them and for you) is to map a reference calendar of notable LGBTQ+ dates and awareness weeks for the upcoming year.

While it might be tempting to give students "free social time" in your classroom during lunch or after school, the lack of *any* kind of structure can make it hard for more socially cautious students to connect with their peers. Try developing a "question of the day," printing out an article, listening to a snippet of a podcast, or developing a short activity to give students a chance to connect to each other and their community as a whole. It doesn't have to be complicated to be effective!

Here's a list, by month, of some notable dates throughout the year that might help to guide you as you build your calendar:

January
International Day to End Conversion Therapy (January 7)
No Name-Calling Week (third week of January)

February
National Black HIV/AIDS Awareness Day (February 7)
Aromantic Spectrum Awareness Week (first full week following Valentine's Day)

March
Bisexual Health Awareness Month (all month)
Zero Discrimination Day (March 1)
National LGBT Health Awareness Week (third week of March)
International Transgender Day of Visibility (March 31)

April
International Asexuality Day (April 6)
Sapphic Visibility Day (April 9)
National Youth HIV/AIDS Awareness Day (April 10)
International Day of Pink (second Wednesday in April)
Day of Silence (second Friday in April)
Nonbinary Parents Day (April 18)
Lesbian Visibility Day (April 26)

May
International Family Equality Day (first Sunday in May)
International Day Against Homophobia, Biphobia and Transphobia (May 17)
Agender Pride Day (May 19)
Harvey Milk Day (May 22)
Pansexual and Panromantic Awareness Day (May 24)

June
LGBTQ+ Pride Month (all month)
LGBTQ Families Day (June 1)
Aromantic Visibility Day (June 5)
HIV Long-Term Survivors Awareness Day (June 5)
Pulse Night of Remembrance (June 12)
Anniversary of Obergefell v. Hodges decision (June 26)
Anniversary of Lawrence v. Texas decision (June 26)

International LGBTQ+ Pride Day (June 28)
Anniversary of the Stonewall Riots (June 28)
Queer Youth of Faith Day (June 30)

July
International Non-Binary People's Day (July 14)
Non-Binary Awareness Week (week of July 14)
International Drag Day (July 16)

August
Transgender History Month (all month)

September
Bisexual Awareness Week (September 16–23)
Celebrate Bisexuality Day (September 23)
National Gay Men's HIV/AIDS Awareness Day (September 27)

October
LGBTQ+ History Month (all month)
International Lesbian Day (October 8)
National Coming Out Day (October 11)
International Pronouns Day (third Wednesday of October)
LGBTQ+ Spirit Day (third Thursday of October)
Genderfluid Visibility Week (October 17–24)
National LGBT Center Awareness Day (October 19)
Intersex Awareness Day (October 26)
Asexual Awareness Week (last full week of October)

November
Transgender Awareness Month (all month)
Transgender Parent Day (first Sunday of November)
Intersex Day of Remembrance (November 8)
Transgender Awareness Week (November 13–19)
Transgender Day of Remembrance (November 20)

December
World AIDS Day (December 1)
Pansexual and Panromantic Pride Day (December 8)
Anniversary of the repeal of "Don't Ask, Don't Tell" (December 18)

Here's an example of how you might choose to organize a calendar of these dates to guide the planning of discussions and events for your campus GSA.

JANUARY

SUNDAY	MONDAY	TUESDAY	WEDNESDAY	THURSDAY	FRIDAY	SATURDAY
					1	2
3	4	5	6	7 INTERNATIONAL DAY TO END CONVERSION THERAPY	8	9
10	11	12	13	14	15	16
17	18 NO NAME-CALLING WEEK	19 NO NAME-CALLING WEEK	20 NO NAME-CALLING WEEK	21 NO NAME-CALLING WEEK	22 NO NAME-CALLING WEEK	23
24/31	25	26	27	28	29	30

FEBRUARY

SUNDAY	MONDAY	TUESDAY	WEDNESDAY	THURSDAY	FRIDAY	SATURDAY
	1	2	3	4	5	6
7 NATIONAL BLACK HIV/AIDS AWARENESS DAY	8	9	10	11	12	13
14	15	16	17	18	19	20
21	22 AROMANTIC SPECTRUM AWARENESS WEEK[1]	23	24	25	26	27
28						

Here are some blank calendar templates you can use to start building plans for your own campus GSA. Happy planning!

SUNDAY	MONDAY	TUESDAY	WEDNESDAY	THURSDAY	FRIDAY	SATURDAY

SUNDAY	MONDAY	TUESDAY	WEDNESDAY	THURSDAY	FRIDAY	SATURDAY

Teaching Like. . .Bali

Pre-Quiz[30]

1. Of the roughly 54.6 million public, private, and charter school students in pre-K through twelfth grade within the United States, what percentage are enrolled in private schools?[31]
   A. 5%
   B. 10%
   C. 15%
   D. 20%
2. According to the Pew Research Center, white students make up just about 47% of traditional public school enrollment in the United States. What is the average enrollment percentage of white students within private schools?
   A. 47%
   B. 55%
   C. 65%
   D. 77%
3. Within the same Pew study, white teachers make up just about 81% of traditional public school staff in the United States. What is the average percentage of white teachers within private schools?
   A. 81%
   B. 83%
   C. 91%
   D. 93%
4. "Out in Black"[32] was a bi-monthly periodical highlighting the lives and stories of North Carolina's Black LGBTQ+ community, and throughout

[30] Answer Key: 1. B, 2. C, 3. B, 4. D.

[31] Schaeffer, Katherine. "U.S. Public, Private and Charter Schools in 5 Charts." Pew Research Center, Pew Research Center, 6 June 2024, www.pewresearch.org/short-reads/2024/06/06/us-public-private-and-charter-schools-in-5-charts/.

[32] "Out in Black: Representations of Black LGBT Individuals in North Carolina · LGBT Identities, Communities, and Resistance in North Carolina, 1945–2012, by David Palmer and His Students · OutHistory." Outhistory.org, OutHistory, 2026, outhistory.org/exhibits/show/nc-lgbt/periodicals/out-in-black-1.

its history, it received subscription requests from readers as far as California, North Korea, and Puerto Rico. In what year was "Out in Black" founded?

A. 1969

B. 1972

C. 1980

D. 1996

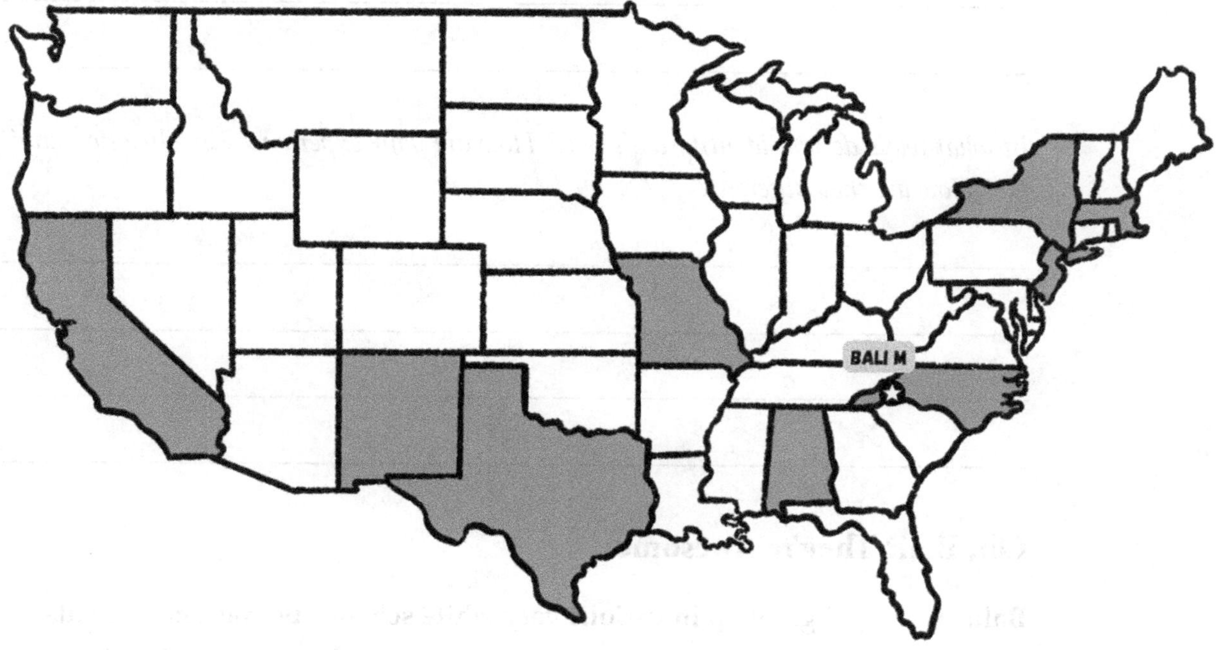

Bali M (they/them)
North Carolina
Private Nonprofit School Director of Equity, Inclusion, and Belonging

Bali (rhymes with "tally" or "rally") was working as a parent educator for a nonprofit when an opportunity arose for them to take on an administrator role at a small private school. As Director of Equity, Inclusion, and Belonging, a position in which Bali has now served for the last five years, they use their experiences as a Black genderqueer educator with a deep passion for justice work to help set the tone for the school as a whole. "I make sure there is an equity lens on everything we do," they say, "and I can pop into different classrooms to be an extra hand. The other week, the third grade teacher was out, so I was the third grade teacher for the day. But my favorite part is teaching our equity elective class, which is something that's required for our middle schoolers to graduate."

Bali is our second educator working out of North Carolina (Stanely being the first). Based on your knowledge and/or assumptions about LGBTQ+ acceptance and protections in North Carolina, what are some of your worries, concerns, and hopes for Bali's experience?

____

____

____

____

In what ways do you identify with Bali? How are your experiences in education similar? How are they different?

____

____

____

____

Oh, Bali? They're Awesome

Bali: **I grew up in various very white schools, because my parents always wanted me in a preparatory school. And not just a private school—it had to have the word "preparatory" in it. And I grew up in a very religious household. So, I feel very strongly that I wasn't able to be myself or even to know that this third category of people existed. For a long time, I was called a "tomboy," but I remember thinking, "I am not a boy! Gross!"**

Flint: Relatable.

Bali: **But I thought, I don't feel very girly either. I think about now, if, for me, there was an adult who loved me and cared enough to say, "These people exist." Not even "you are one," but "Hey, there are genderqueer people around. It's a thing," you know? That would have mattered a lot to me. I needed a different message about gay people too. That would have been really great. As an adult, that would have helped my teenage mental health a lot.**

Flint: I feel like so many queer people look back and wish there was an adult version of themselves to help the kid in us who deserved more.

Bali: And people assume that when we talk about equity education and gender education that we're going around to kids saying "You are trans! And you are trans!" in the Oprah Winfrey voice.

Flint: Look under your seat—it's a new gender!

Bali: That's just not what's happening. What's actually happening is that when I introduce myself, especially to the younger grades, I say "Hey, my name is Bali. My pronouns are they/them. That just means I am a person, not a girl. You might look at me and you might think I am a girl, but I'm not. And so instead of saying, 'Oh, Bali? She's awesome', you would say 'Oh, Bali? They're awesome'." And that's it. I exist.

Flint: That's such a great and easy frame, too. You're giving an example of how to use your pronouns, you're explaining what it means, and it's not super complicated. You had said at some point that kids generally "get it." Has that been your experience?

Bali: Yeah, they're just like, "Oh, a new kind of person! Great!" When you are a kid, you're just collecting all kinds of new people all the time.

Flint: That's like at least 90% of being a kid, that's true.

Bali: Back in the 2023–2024 school year, I asked this queer group of students how they feel about equity education here. And this one student said:

"I think it's important to go to a gender-affirming school because it can really boost a kid's confidence in themselves. And especially with early education, it really can back up anything they may believe and not know about yet. I think it's important because this way it's not coming from a big blob of people and it normalizes it so that it's not seen as this big breaker. Because it's not that people are forcing it on children; it's that they're actually learning and the world isn't just black and white. So I think it's important to be able to give that kind of space to a kid so they can understand, help themselves and others with it. And it can prevent any later on depression or things that may stem from not having that early care about it."

And that was an eighth grader.

Flint: An eighth grader?

Bali: Yeah

Flint: Wow. Well, I'll look out for her presidential bid soon.

Much of the discomfort around "they/them" pronouns can stem from a lack of practice. Imagine you were introducing Bali to a student or colleague and rehearse your introduction here.

____

____

____

____

What kinds of adult narratives or validation would have improved your own experience as a growing child? How can we step in as that kind of an adult in our lives and school communities now?

____

____

____

____

Guess Who

Flint: You mentioned that once every other quarter or so, you teach an equity elective, and it's a requirement for graduation for your eighth graders. Can you tell me a bit about what that class looks like?

Bali: So, that class focuses primarily on racial justice. But, what's really important to me is that I never tell my students what to think—I want them to develop critical thinking skills. A lot of the activities have them reading something, digesting it, and then an activity where they have to talk amongst themselves about it while using quotes and examples from the text.

Flint: My English teacher heart is going pitter-patter.

Bali: I always want the focus to be: how do we talk to each other about difficult subjects? How do we come to our own conclusions? And we can't do that without a little bit of media literacy. We might do something as simple as look at the pictures selected for different articles about the same subject or event.

Flint: Oh, that's a good one.

Bali: Right? Because oftentimes, what do we look at? We look at the picture and we look at the headline, and that's it. So I ask, "If I want to have a positive view on something, what picture do you think I would use? If I wanted to have a negative view, how would that change?"

Flint: Helping them not accept everything at face value. That's an important lesson.

Bali: My favorite part of the class is at the beginning, because we start with a "Guess Who" tournament. Usually, what ends up happening is the kid who asks, "Is your person Black? Is your person white?" They're usually the champion, because that helps you with half the board, easily.

Flint: Ah, I think I get it.

Bali: Yep, because race doesn't have to be a heavy thing to talk about. Oftentimes, we're taught "don't talk about race" and "be colorblind," and that's not helpful all the time.

Flint: So you're sort of starting in a more covert way, breaking the ice by talking about race and ethnicity in a way that's a little bit disarming, right?

Bali: So they're not coming in with their walls up about it, yeah.

How would you feel using any of the activities inspired by Bali's equity class? Which would be the easiest to adapt for you? Which would make you the most nervous? Why?

____

____

____

____

When It's Time for a Policy

Flint: So, as a Black genderqueer administrator in a pretty white school, how do issues of identity factor into the way that you move through your job?

Bali: I have to be very strategic about how I handle certain conversations with parents, which is in a different way than with children. The children are so easy. The children want to talk. But parents are the ones that don't want to offend me, but they also have issues, so sometimes they just won't talk to me at all. And that's really difficult, because my job is to talk to people.

Luckily, my [administrator] team is great. They'll talk to me about it if they hear about an issue from a parent. I am not explicitly excluded, but maybe I am not in the room when that conversation happens, because the parent specifically went to somebody else when they probably should have come to me.

Flint: Yikes. And what's that like?

Bali: It's awkward, but my team is always saying, "You should really talk to Bali about this."

Flint: How often do you think they take that advice?

Bali: I think a good number of times I will get a parent who reaches out to me after that, even if it's hard for them. There are some parents, though, who are too far over that fence, and they won't. And then, do they usually stay at the school? No.

Flint: See now that's interesting and something I hadn't considered. My experience is all public education, right? People don't just leave. Like, this is where your kid's going. This is such a different dynamic. You might end up with a parent that chooses to remove their kid from the school if they're uncomfy about something, right?

Bali: At one point, when I first started, we had a pretty decent size group of students who called themselves the "queer group." It highlighted an institutional lack of clarity for us, because some of them would change their names and their pronouns,

which is adolescence, you know? But some families and staff were asking for a policy.

Flint: Ah.

Bali: I don't love policies, because once you put something in a policy, that's the way it has to be, without much flexibility. And so we found out that, years before I got there, the school had already introduced a policy. So, what we did was reintroduce that same policy.

Flint: And what happened then?

Bali: We had someone who left the school. They felt uncomfortable, and they had the right to leave, but it felt pretty bad.

Flint: Wow. And what was the policy?

Bali: It was essentially that on official records, we have to put whatever name is on the birth certificate. But things like gender-segregated activities? We don't do that. We also won't do a "boys" and a "girls" line. We'll use inclusive language. We won't deadname somebody if a student comes to us and tells us that they're trans, and we're not going to necessarily "out" them to their parents. What we're going to do is connect that student with the counselor with family permission and find the best way to handle this, and our hope is always to be the bridge from home to school and from school to home. We recognize that's going to look different for each kid, and so we're going to go by what the counselor recommends.

Flint: So, was the parent mad because it wasn't inclusive enough or because it was too inclusive?

Bali: Too inclusive.

Do you agree with Bali's perspective regarding "policies"? Why or why not?

____

____

How do the dynamics of a private school complicate equity work and allyship? In what ways might the work be easier, and how might it be harder? How do you know?

____

____

____

____

Double Whammy of Identities

Bali: **Sometimes, when we talk about queer issues, we tend to forget that BIPOC[33] also exist in that space, and they're getting hit with the double whammy of identities. And then you throw in neurodiversity? There are so many other intersections, and we can't forget that. I feel like we do sometimes. Those students can feel forgotten in one identity or the other.**

Flint: Yeah, you might feel like you have to just "pick one," but that's not how it works.

Bali: **When people talk about these issues, they tend to talk about them in buckets. There's the neurodiversity movement, and then there's issues in Black communities and issues in queer communities. Very frequently, you're talking about the same person across all of these different places.**

Flint: Do you feel like there is more that could be done for educators with a lot of these intersecting identities to feel more comfortable and more accepted and more safe in schools?

Bali: **I think that that's a job of administration, because I see it as a culture issue. The staff and students are definitely part of forming that culture, but it really takes the boundaries of leadership to affirm the walls of that culture and show what is and is not permitted or accepted.**

Flint: If you've got a principal in front of you who's trying to create this culture, is there an immediate thought that you have about what they could be doing, probably better than they're doing now?

Bali: **Having a shared vocabulary is a big one, I think.**

Flint: Wait, yes, say more about that.

[33] An acronym meaning "Black, Indigenous, and People of Color," pronounced "bye-pock."

Bali: **Like, are you afraid to say "white supremacy"? Are you afraid to say "queer"? And is it because people have different thoughts about what white supremacy is? Because yeah, people will have different thoughts, but presenting a shared vocabulary allows for the organization to be on the same page when discussing various topics. And also, do you have equity-based trainings that you participate in? Are they required for your staff?**

Flint: There it is. That's the one.

Bali: **If you are touring with families, do you talk about the equity work being done within the school? And, again, I'm coming from a private school. Are you having parents sign on for enrollment, but they don't know the equity work that you do in that school? These are things that can help shape the culture.**

Flint: It seems like so much of this is coming back to fear. Are you afraid of engaging with this work? Are you afraid of other people knowing that you're engaging with this work?

Bali: **Are you afraid of losing that family? Yeah.**

Flint: Right? If you're worried about your enrollment, are you willing to let your spine dissolve when it gets harder?

Take a moment to reflect on Bali's perspectives around the role of school administrators. They say, "It really takes the boundaries of leadership to affirm the walls of that [school] culture." To what extent do you agree or disagree?

____

____

____

____

The Parents We Listen To

Bali: **You always have to ask—what families are you listening to?**

Flint: Mmhmm, yeah.

Bali: **And notice which parents are showing up more. As an administrator, that's part of your role.**

Flint: It's rare to hear people talking about this, but it's so influential in school culture, and you're 120% right about it. You should say it all the time as loud as possible. Yes.

Bali:	**You have to be curious—who are you making time for? Why do *they* have the time? Because, I get it. We're tired. I'm tired. But maybe once a week, every other week, can you make time to take phone calls after 5 p.m.? There are people who can't get in touch because they don't have the time.**
Flint:	Schools everywhere—private, public, charter—so much of it is ruled by parents and families. So, who's being listened to? Who's at school board meetings? Who's in your office? Who's at the PTA? Does your school have a PTA?
Bali:	**We call it the Parent Council.**
Flint:	When does the Parent Council meet?
Bali:	**Not at a great time. It's at nine in the morning.**
Flint:	Yeah, so that's who's going to show up, right? It's going to be who is available at 9 a.m. on a Friday. Who can afford to be home? Is it mostly moms?
Bali:	**Of course. So now you have to have a dual-parent home, and they have to have enough money for mom to be there. It would have to be someone who does not have a 9-to-5. Yep. I am 100% aware, and I can only push so much. Because, for now, that's the time the Parent Council President can meet, and that's the time that is available. We've tried various times and people didn't show up, but again, that lands, I feel like, on us.**

Is there a family or parent group with routine meetings within your school community? When do they meet? Who is represented, and who is not?

____

____

What are the potential consequences that can stem from an inaccessible family group?

____

____

What are some possible solutions?

____

____

The Internal Work

Bali: **A lot of getting rid of the fear within this work is doing your own work. It's a spiritual thing.**

Flint: Yeah, absolutely.

Bali: **That's why I turn off the news. I have to be somewhat aware of the news, but I know when I have to pause it because I can get compassion fatigue. A lot of it is inner work, and if you are not ready to do inner work, you are not ready to do equity work.**

Flint: Oof, that's exactly it.

Bali: **Because all of the trauma from all of the "-isms," all of the "-phobias," it lives in our DNA, and if we are not ready to work through it, we can't help that little kid as much as we want.**

Flint: What does that look like for you?

Bali: **Journaling. I really like collaging when I have the time. I'll go to the library and get all those free magazines. Spending time with family. Sometimes I just have to turn my brain off and watch some anime. So much is doing things that don't necessarily cost money, because I feel like "self-care" has taken on this capitalistic tone. I'll go running even though sometimes I hate running, but it's free. I can do it right outside my door, and by the time I come back, I am like, "Okay. I've gotten that out of my body."**

Flint: You need a physical way, I get that. You have to get this stuff out somehow. I think some educators think "self-care" means a bath bomb and a spa weekend, but sometimes you just have to remember that you have a body, right? And remember that you're a person with a sense of self outside of what you do.

Take a moment to reflect on this sentence: "If you are not ready to do inner work, you are not ready to do equity work." Do you agree? Why or why not?

____

____

____

____

Let's Recap:

What sticks out to you about Bali's experiences? What are your overall reflections for this chapter?

____

____

____

____

What questions do you still have?

____

____

Teaching Like. . .Janelle

Pre-Quiz[34]

1. According to the 2024 National Assessment of Educational Progress (NAEP[35]) data, New Mexico ranks where in fourth and eighth grade reading and mathematics, when compared to the rest of the country?
   A. 25th
   B. 45th
   C. 50th
   D. 52nd
2. According to research from the Trevor Project,[36] what percentage of LGBTQ+ students enrolled in middle or high school reported being bullied either in person or electronically in the past year?
   A. 24%
   B. 41%
   C. 52%
   D. 60%

[34] Answer Key: 1. D, 2. C, 3. B, 4. B.

[35] "Understanding Results | NAEP." Nces.ed.gov, nces.ed.gov/nationsreportcard/guides/.

[36] The Trevor Project. "Bullying and Suicide Risk Among LGBTQ Youth." The Trevor Project, 14 Oct 2021, www.thetrevorproject.org/research-briefs/bullying-and-suicide-risk-among-lgbtq-youth/.

3. Which of the following is **not** a tier within Maslow's Hierarchy of Needs?
   A. Physiological needs
   B. Housing needs
   C. Love and belonging
   D. Self-actualization
4. True or false: New Mexico has standards that require social studies curriculum to be inclusive of LGBTQ+ contributions throughout history.
   A. True
   B. False

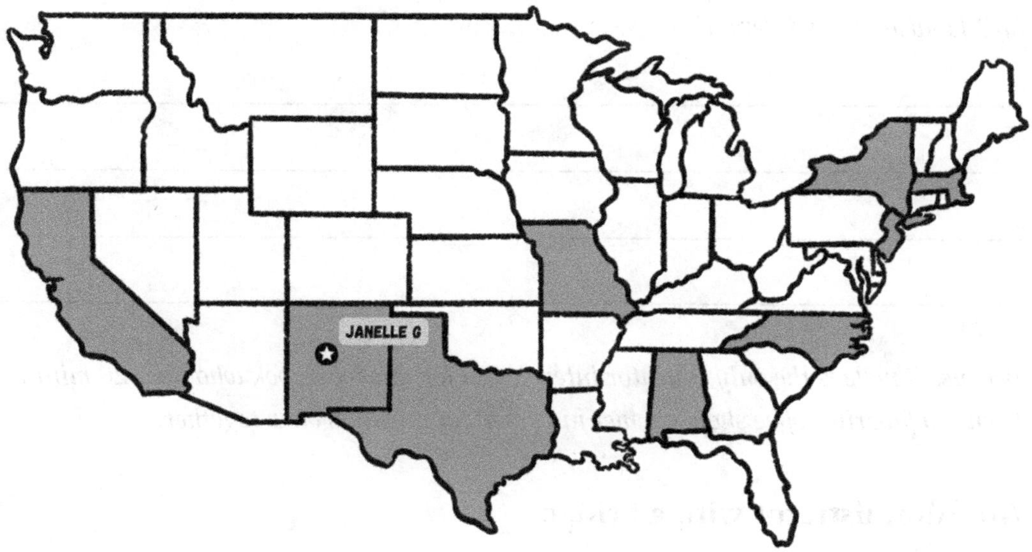

Janelle G (she/her)
New Mexico
Communications Director for the New Mexico Public Education Department

Across her more than 32 years within education, Nuevo Mexicana/Hispana educator Janelle has worn many hats. She's been a first grade teacher, bilingual programs director, cheer coach, assistant professor, assistant principal, and is now the communications director for the New Mexico Public Education Department. And though she's accomplished much, including starting a charter school and creating an entire Navajo language curriculum, she still lists the lasting relationships she's built with students as her most treasured accomplishment. "I'm that mama bear, and I'm going to protect my kids," she says, "and that includes my students."

Based on your knowledge and/or assumptions about LGBTQ+ acceptance and protections in New Mexico, what are some of your worries, concerns, and hopes for Janelle's experience?

____

____

____

____

In what ways do you identify with Janelle? How are your experiences in education similar? How are they different?

____

____

____

____

Because Janelle is the only educator interviewed for this workbook who lives 20 minutes from my favorite coffee shop, we met in person for our interview together.

An Administrator with a Fridge

Janelle: **I loved being an assistant principal at a high school, because I felt like I was a safe haven for a lot of kids for a lot of different reasons. I was that person. I kept a little fridge in my office.**

Flint: We love an administrator with a fridge.

Janelle: **It was always string cheese, crackers, and water. Kids knew they could just come in. It got to the point where they'd just come in, grab what they needed, and walk out. I still have kids to this day—gosh, I was talking to one the other day—and they told me they were 38 now. I'm thinking, oh my God, I've known you since you were 14.**

Flint: Yeah, that's always a wild surprise, isn't it?

Janelle: **Some of them will still see me and call me "mom." I've taught elementary and then I was the administrator at a high school, and really, the big kids have the same exact needs as little first graders. They need nurturing and mentoring, and they need safety. I may cry here at some point, because—see, I'm already starting.**

Flint: [offers a tissue]

Janelle: No thanks, I have one. See, we only had school four days a week. We didn't have school on Fridays. We knew a lot of our kids—we were in a low socioeconomic and high-needs area—many of them had to work. We thought if we have a four-day school week, they're still going to get in all of their required curriculum, but they'll have another chance to work or whatever it is they need to do.

Flint: That makes sense, yeah.

Janelle: So, I had a big group of kids, primarily boys, that would come to the school on Fridays anyway. Staff still had professional development and meetings and things on Fridays, so the school was open. One day some boys came in and I asked, "What are you guys doing here? It's Friday, you have the day off." And they said, "Well, Miss, this doesn't feel like school to me anymore. You feel like home."

Flint: Wow.

Janelle: And it wasn't "the *school* feels like home"; it was "*you* feel like home." That was the best compliment I think I could ever get. They wanted to be there. How many kids would want to be at school, you know? But I just thought, who knows what they're dealing with at home? They thought this was the place they'd rather be on a Friday morning, when they could be home sleeping. But, they wanted to be near us, you know? I'll never forget that.

Janelle mentions that "big kids" have the same needs as first-graders. Do you agree with her? Why or why not?

___

___

___

___

What do you think Janelle's student meant when he said, "You feel like home"? What need was school likely filling for him? What can all adults within a school community be doing to "feel like home"?

____

____

____

____

An Appleseed in the Desert

Janelle: **I put out a press release a couple of weeks ago, because we have a new program with a local nonprofit called New Mexico Appleseed. What they did with this small pilot—it was something like 14 students [experiencing housing insecurity]—is they paid them $500 a month as an incentive to attend school and turn in their homework, but they also had to meet with a financial counselor and a guidance counselor. It was trying to target students who were homeless or about to become homeless.**

Flint: I don't know if I've ever heard of a program like that before.

Janelle: **Right? The question was, if we give you $500, is that going to help you graduate from high school? Fourteen out of the 15 students graduated.**

Flint: That's incredible.

Janelle: **Yes, and so now, in this last legislative session, we just got $2.1 million appropriated for the project. The *Washington Post* picked up the story, ran it, and now we're doing it with about 330 students throughout the state, within 12 different schools. Students are going to get a debit card, $500 a month for attending school and making sure their grades stay up—there's all these criteria. But I was reading the comments [on the *Washington Post* article], and it's like, wow, a lot of these people are finding out that New Mexico really has some great things going. Everyone looks at NAEP[37] scores, and they say we're 50th, but I think we have so much more to offer than that. We have universal childcare now. We have universal pre-K. We have free college.**

[37] The National Assessment of Educational Progress.

Flint: I've been starting to learn about the social programs in the state now that we live here, and it feels like the list gets longer every day.

Janelle: There's so much. Any student who graduates from a New Mexico high school can go to college for free. And now we're incentivizing homeless students to try to get them out of that poverty cycle. New Mexico has some wonderful things going on. When I was in our policy department at the public education department, I was working with the Transgender Resource Center of New Mexico to write protections for trans students in New Mexico public schools.

Flint: Is that something that's been paused?

Janelle: It's been put on the back burner, unfortunately, but it's something I worked on for like two solid years. We were trying to codify, in law, that civil rights protections are for everybody, including LGBTQ+ students in schools, which means "Don't touch our libraries, don't touch our books, let our teachers fly rainbow flags, let them have 'ally' stickers on their classroom doors"—that kind of thing.

Flint: Those are rights we're seeing attacked in a lot of other places.

Janelle: Yes, exactly. In other states, we've seen that all that stuff has gotten people fired. We haven't codified it in law yet, but I think New Mexico is just very special in that we are trying.

Flint: We're trying.

Janelle: We, unfortunately, still have our pockets of people who are nasty and don't want to see all kids succeed. But, I think, we have a lot of positive things happening. We have allies everywhere. I've talked to families who have moved into the state so that their LGBTQ+ children will be more protected.

Flint: So, it's not all handled, but we're also not making steps in the wrong direction.

Janelle: Exactly, exactly.

Flint: What's fascinating, right, is that even if you haven't gotten some of these protections written into the law yet, these other ones that you're talking about—free college, having these preventative measures to help students who are experiencing homelessness, child care, all of those—help queer people too.

> They can fill some gaps, these support structures that tend to exist in homes where you have a lot of support. Any time your state can help cover some of what a supportive and resourced family should be doing, that's helping queer people too.

What are your initial reactions to learning about the New Mexico Appleseed project?

____

____

____

____

State NAEP scores are determined by results from a congressionally-mandated large-scale assessment that is most frequently reported in fourth and eighth grade across the subjects of mathematics, reading, and science. What purpose should scores like these serve, if any? What are the benefits and consequences of a nationwide education "report card"?

____

____

____

____

Take a moment to reflect on the statement "Any time your state can help cover some of what a supportive and resourced family should be doing, that's helping queer people too." What does that mean? Why might non-LGBTQ+ social programs still benefit LGBTQ+ populations?

____

____

____

____

Maslow's Hierarchy of Needs

Flint: The students you've had over the course of your career—what do you think it is that you've done that creates that energy, that vibe? What makes students trust you, do you think?

Janelle: **It's at least partially because I'm an open book. Everybody knows everything about me. My first marriage was very abusive—physically, mentally, verbally, everything. So when I would have instances where I'd hear that girls were having issues with their boyfriend or somebody saw somebody slap somebody or pull somebody's hair, I would share my own story with these girls. I'd tell them, "That's not acceptable. Don't make the mistake I made." Every other month I was getting rushed to the emergency room because I had a broken rib or I had a punctured lung. I would tell them, "These things have happened to me, but I've been able to survive them. I got therapy."**

Flint: Wow, thank you for sharing that.

Janelle: **I've always been my authentic self with students, and I don't have a lot of secrets. I feel comfortable enough with myself that everybody knows my story. I think it's important for people to know that I might have a PhD, but I still grew up on the streets of this town. I've gotten into fights, and I've been suspended from school. I am who I am, and I'm willing to stand up for people.**

Flint: You definitely seem like someone I'd want in my corner. Do you think there are any other reasons why students have seen you as a safe person for them?

Janelle: **Well, I always have food. The kids knew they could count on me for juice and a breakfast burrito. Maybe those boys came to see me on Fridays just because they were hungry, you know?**

Flint: I was that classroom, too. I had food constantly, and I got criticized a lot by people who were saying things like, "You shouldn't be spending your money in your classroom." But I think there's a hierarchy of needs, and a kid can't learn if they're hungry. A kid can't do anything, really, if they're hungry, or if they're cold, or if they don't feel like they have a place they can be safe. Sometimes providing those really basic needs first is what makes it possible for them to connect.

Janelle: **Right. And if we're talking Maslow's Hierarchy of Needs, you're fulfilling just that very little one. There might be others you could probably help them fulfill. There were lots of times where I would tell kids, "Why don't we write in your IEP?[38] That you need to talk to a social worker? And when you're feeling like you can't function in class, you have permission to go to a social worker."**

Flint: Sometimes they're just getting a little bit of evidence that somebody cares about any part of them. It's powerful to find out that someone is willing to, like you said, fight for them or feed them a string cheese.

Janelle: **And lots of times, these boys would just come in to sit at my table and cry. Because it was okay for them to be male and come in and just cry. And they didn't have to tell me anything. I had built this safe space for them that said "if you're hungry, you can come in here. If you're upset, you can come in here. If you're sad about something or depressed about something, you can come in here." And I'm not going to ask questions until you want to talk to me about it.**

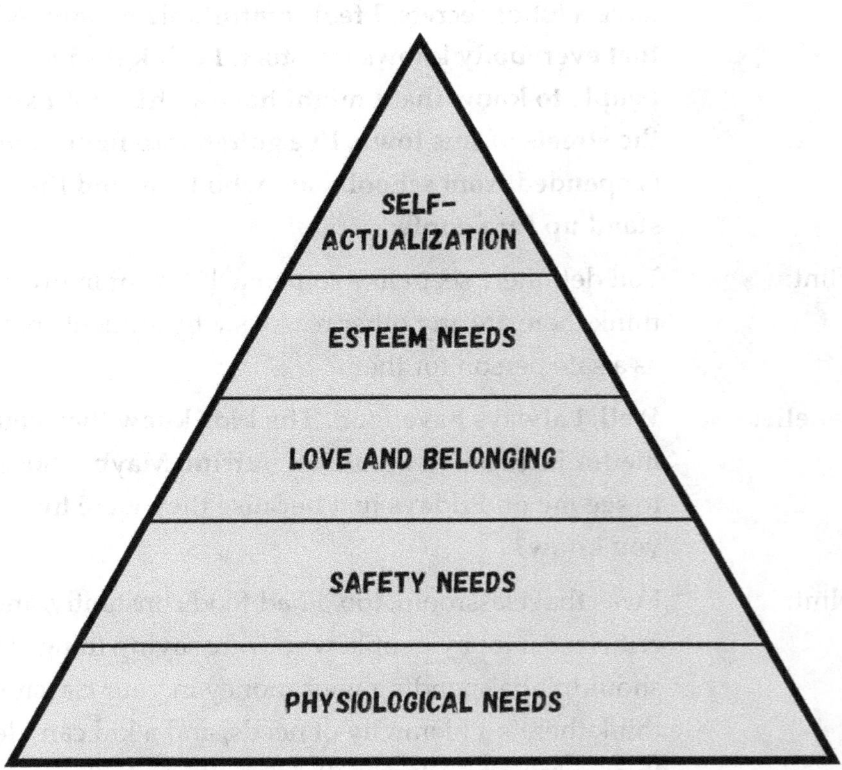

[38] Individualized education program.

This pyramid represents Maslow's Hierarchy of Needs. Using your own understanding and/or research, fill in each section with your understanding of the needs that fit within each category.

Reference the Maslow's Hierarchy of Needs graphic as you answer this question: on what level of this pyramid do we hope our students have access when they come to school each day? Why? What barriers might keep them from reaching it?

____

____

____

____

Janelle mentions that part of her strategy for connecting with students was to be an "open book" about her own life and experiences. Is there a part of you resistant to that particular strategy, either for yourself or your colleagues in education? Why or why not?

____

____

____

____

We're Kind of Dealing with the Kid Locked in the Bathroom Right Now

Flint: You have two sons, and one of them, you said, is gay, and that growing up in this area was a challenge for him?

Janelle: Oh, yeah.

Flint: Are you willing to share what that experience was like?

Janelle: Oh, now you're really going to make me cry.

Flint: No pressure at all. We don't have to talk about it if you don't want to.

Janelle: No, I do. It's really part of who I am.

My husband and I kind of figured it out when he was three, but he didn't come out to us until he was almost finished with high school. We've always been comfortable with who he is, but we started noticing that he was having a lot of mental

health struggles in middle school. And I think middle school is horrible for any kid anyway, like every parent should be paid to keep their kids home for three years, sixth through eighth grade, and deal with them themselves and then let them go back into the world. Middle school is one age I've never taught.

Flint: It's a one-way ticket to heaven to be a middle school teacher.

Janelle: Yep. So, that's when I saw him struggling the most. I started noticing he was getting really angry. Boys would go by and just throw all the books off his desk, and the school wouldn't do anything about the bullying. I ended up, thank God, filing a formal complaint with the state, because he had an IEP. I said, "You're not taking care of his mental health and his social needs by allowing all these kids to bully him."

Flint: Man, that's just horrible.

Janelle: And I'd call the school or go meet with the principal, and she would say, "I reprimanded them, but I can't tell you what the reprimand is." Really? If that's true, how come the next day they're back at it again? For three years I fought and I fought and I fought with that school. My husband jokes and says, "The superintendent has your face, and they throw darts at you every day," because I once applied for a job at that office and didn't get it.

Flint: Yeah, you're on the blacklist for sure.

Janelle: This man hates me. And he's like this 5'5" guy, so I purposely wear big heels every time I have to meet with him, because he was such an asshole.

Flint: [laughs]

Janelle: But as my son started growing bigger, the bullying stopped. They knew he wasn't going to take crap. He's a lot like his mother.

Flint: I bet.

Janelle: But like I said, he still never fully came out to us until his senior year in high school.

Flint: And how did that happen?

Janelle: Well, our younger son was on the freshman football team. He was little. He's an August birthday, so he was a lot smaller than the other boys. He wasn't getting playing time. So, unbeknownst to us, he was telling us he was at practice, but instead he'd go hide in the auditorium and wait for his brother to take him home. He was afraid to tell us he'd quit.

Flint: Oh no! Poor baby.

Janelle: And so we went to a scrimmage, and we're there looking for him, and we're like, "I don't see number 67. Where is he?" We get home and I'm calling his phone and I ask him, "Where are you?" When he finally gets home, he locks himself in the bathroom, and my husband and I are trying to figure out what's going on, right?

And then [older son], in order to save his brother from whatever he thought he was going to experience, just walked into our bedroom and said, "I'm gay."

Flint: [laughs] Oh, boy.

Janelle: And we're like, "Okay, we love and accept you, but we're kind of dealing with the kid locked in the bathroom right now."

Flint: He saw his opportunity and he took it.

Janelle: Yeah, that was his opportunity.

Flint: I'm sure, for both of them, there's this worry that you're going to disappoint your parents. Even if they haven't given you the evidence that that's true, there's still that feeling.

Janelle: Absolutely. And now like he's almost 30, and he's found his niche; he found his people.

Flint: Any hopes for him now?

Janelle: Well, I do want him to date more.

What steps should the school and district have taken against bullying in the case of Janelle's son? Whose responsibility is his safety at school? Why?

____

____

____

____

Within the LGBTQ+ community, it is exceptionally common for a person to "come out" to their parents only after they've come out to others. Why do you think that is?

____

____

____

____

Let's Recap:

What sticks out to you about Janelle's experiences? What are your overall reflections for this chapter?

____

____

____

____

What questions do you still have?

____

____

____

____

Teaching Like. . .Katherine

Pre-Quiz[39]

1. The United Nations "Convention on the Rights of the Child," a document outlining international law regarding universal child-specific needs and rights, was adopted by the UN General Assembly in 1989. To date, 196 countries are party to the UNCRC, including every member nation of the UN aside from one. Which country played an active role in the drafting of the Convention but has not ratified it?
   A. Saudi Arabia
   B. Ireland
   C. India
   D. The United States of America
2. Which of these is *not* a right outlined within the Convention on the Rights of the Child?
   A. The right to a life free from violence
   B. The right to nondiscrimination
   C. The right to access education
   D. The right to freedom from child labor

[39] Answer Key: 1. D, 2. D, 3. A, 4. C.

3. State family leave laws, which decide whether a person can take leave from work to care for a child, do not always allow for parental recognition within same-sex relationships. All of the following states *lack* an inclusive parental leave law *except for*. . .

   A. Nevada

   B. New Mexico

   C. Alabama

   D. North Carolina

   E. New Hampshire

4. Alabama's House Bill 322 bans transgender students from using bathrooms and other school facilities that align with their gender identity and also bans any acknowledgment of sexual orientation or gender identity in classrooms from kindergarten through fifth grade. In what year did the Alabama State Senate pass H.B. 322?

   A. 1969

   B. 1999

   C. 2022

   D. 2025

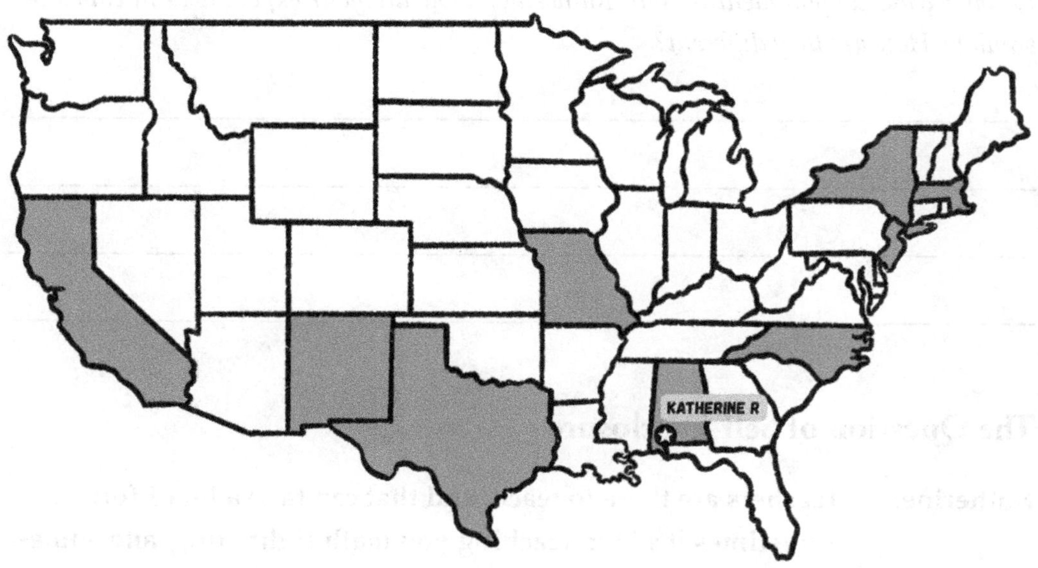

Katherine R (she/her)
Alabama
Elementary School Counselor

After she became a mother, seven-year-veteran school counselor Katherine was faced with a choice: return to the school where she'd spent half a decade building relationships with the students who loved and trusted her, or leave the world of public education for good? As a queer woman in the Deep South who'd become disillusioned by the systems keeping her students in cycles of poverty (along with a counselor-to-student ratio of 1 to 700), she made the impossible choice to leave her school for good, though she knows how important her role was while she was there. "I might not have been the perfect counselor," she says, "but I could build a really strong relationship with kids really fast. . .I loved it."

Based on your knowledge and/or assumptions about LGBTQ+ acceptance and protections in Alabama, what are some of your worries, concerns, and hopes for Katherine's experience?

____

____

____

____

In what ways do you identify with Katherine? How are your experiences in education similar? How are they different?

____

____

____

____

The Question of Self-Disclosure

Katherine: **Teachers are there to teach, and that can take a lot of forms. Sometimes it's "I'm teaching you math right now," and sometimes it's life lessons, right? Teachers, often, fill in a space for kids who don't have anybody else.**

Flint: I'd say that's accurate, yeah.

Katherine: **As a counselor, it felt stickier. Because not only am I gay, but also kids open up in a different way when they understand what counseling is or what they think it should be. They get in that room, and it's much more private than a classroom. You've got the little twinkle lights, quiet music, and they know you're a safe person, so they just sort of pour it out.**

Flint: I imagine that happens much faster, yeah.

Katherine: **My kids know right away, unless they tell me something where someone's getting hurt, I'm never going to tell anyone what they say. Teachers don't come in with that. That's a disclaimer I have to make as a counselor. Once they trusted me, they would open up, and I felt like I had to be very careful where I stepped, right?**

Flint: What do you mean?

Katherine: **When you're learning to be a counselor, they teach you in school that self-disclosure is bad. As a teacher, sometimes you can self-disclose and it makes sense—that's fair. But you don't want to go in a session with a counselor who's going to talk about themselves the whole time, right? That's not what I'm here for.**

Flint: There are different opinions about self-disclosure in therapy and counseling spaces, though, right? In some ways, that's changing?

Katherine: **Yeah, and maybe this is weird to say, but it's almost a heteronormative way of viewing counseling? Queer people know—and I'm sure this is true for many marginalized people—that it's often super important for a counselor to say, "I see you." And I don't mean "I see you from afar," but "I've been there with you."**

Flint: It's a pretty critical part of safety for us, yeah.

Katherine: **I always felt this tension when I was in school about self-disclosure. So the question became, especially with kids, "Am I disclosing for me or for them?"**

Flint: Oh, wait, that seems like a really helpful internal guideline.

Katherine: **And it can still be really hard to figure out sometimes, especially as someone who is a big "sharer." It's a lot of the way that I connect with people. It was just a tough thing to**

navigate: how much of myself do I reveal? Because there were some moments where kids would come out to me, and I didn't think it was appropriate for me to say, "Oh, me too." I just listened to them.

Flint: That's what a lot of kids need, I expect.

Katherine: There were other times, though, where they told me and I knew I did need to tell them, especially when shame would come up. "I'll never be a good person," or "I'll never have a family," or "I'm going to go to hell." So many of these kids could not see themselves as an adult. That's when it's time for me to say, "You see this person in my picture right here? That's my wife."

Flint: Okay, so I might cry.

Katherine: It would absolutely blow their minds. You could see all of those gears clicking into place where they're realizing "I could be a teacher?" or "I could have a house and a family?" Because these kids are not living in Portland, you know? They're not seeing queer adults who feel comfortable in public interacting or holding hands. They may have never seen a queer adult ever, outside of maybe TV.

Flint: Wow.

Katherine: And every time I said it, I knew there was a chance that they would turn around, go home, and say, "I went to see the counselor today, and she told me she's gay."

Flint: That fear, that hypervigilance, is always there. Yeah.

Katherine: I'm always thinking, "Today is the day that I think I'm doing the right thing, and I get fired." But I told my principal early on, I said, "I will not lie. I will not lie to these kids. If they ask me a direct question, I'm going to tell them the truth. And you can either back me up or not, but I don't want this job if I have to lie to kids."

Make a "T" chart listing the potential pros and cons of self-disclosure for school counselors.

Would the pros and cons you've listed be different from the same considerations for teachers? Why or why not?

Katherine is a counselor in a part of the United States often called "the Deep South." What does that change, if anything, in regard to your answer for the previous question?

Y'all Aren't Counselors

Katherine: **The theme for my job has always been balance—a balance between laws and children's needs, but also my own needs as a queer person. There has to be a balance also, which is really difficult, between laws, district rules, and district standards versus my Bible as a counselor: the American School Counselor Association's ethical framework.**

Flint: Can you say more about that?

Katherine: **The ASCA's framework is, to me, incredibly clear. They say that all students have the right to equitable access to the**

school counselor, who supports them, advocates for and affirms them regardless of, but not limited to. . .and then it lists all the things. Very specifically, on that list, they didn't just put "sexual orientation." They put "sexual orientation, gender identity, gender expression, and family type."

Flint: Yeah, I'd say that's pretty clear.

Katherine: Yes, and a lot of times, the things that I was being told at a state and local level directly conflicted with my ethical standards. But when it comes to state laws versus ethical standards, I'm going with the ethical standards. You can come after me if you want.

Flint: Truly, the kind of bravery our students deserve.

Katherine: And that same framework says all students have the right to information and the support needed to enhance their self-development and affirmation within one's group identities. Kids have a right to have information. And it doesn't say "only if they're above 18." All kids have a right to age-appropriate access to this information.

Flint: It's not a right you see being supported everywhere right now, that's for sure.

Katherine: And it's critical. Self-hatred can be so strong when you have no one to lean on. You're not going home, usually, to a family of other gay people. Often, you're going home to straight people who don't understand you. So whenever those state laws or our district policies counteract what's being told to me within those ethical standards? I'm sorry, I'm going with the ethical standards. Y'all aren't counselors; you're people trying to protect yourself from lawsuits.

A "moral injury" is defined as the profound spiritual and psychological distress that results from acting against your deeply held internal values system. In what ways are educators confronted with moral injury? What should we do about it, if anything?

___

___

___

___

The Children's Bill of Rights

Katherine: **I worked with students between 5 and 12 years old, and here's the thing: even middle schoolers have a little bit of control in their lives, right? High schoolers have even more. Kids under 12 are oppressed by their situation. I will always and forever believe that kids are the most oppressed minority.**

Flint: Wait, tell me more.

Katherine: **Imagine on top of all of the other demographic labels you can add to someone in this country and then add "child." You would not want to be in that position, right? I guess people on the political left tend to miss "kids" as one of the most crucial oppressed groups.**

Flint: We, famously, don't have a "children' s bill of rights" the way a lot of other countries do.

Katherine: **That is a hill that I will die on and another reason why I won't go back to public education. I believe they continue to oppress kids. I spent a lot of my time begging adults to stop oppressing children, and they always seemed confused.**

Flint: I can understand that. We remember what it was like—or at least, I think a lot of us remember what it was like—to be a kid and to have so little control over your life. So many of us turn around and do the same thing to children.

> *The United Nations Convention on the Rights of the Child, adopted by the UN General Assembly in 1989, is an agreement held by 196 countries promising to protect children's rights across the globe. The United States is currently the only nation within the UN who is not party to it, though they were instrumental in its drafting.*
>
> *Within the text of the UNCRC, there are 42 universal rights and definitions outlined as inalienable for every child protected by international law. The United Nations Children's Fund (UNICEF[40]) has published a list of the rights highlighted in the UNCRC in simplified, "child-friendly" accessible language (aptly named "The Children's Version").*

[40] "Child Rights Connect." Child Rights Connect, `childrightsconnect.org/`.

Though I won't be able to publish the entire list within this pages of this workbook, here is a selection of some of those rights:

#3. When adults make decisions, they should think about how their decisions will affect children. All adults should do what is best for children. Governments should make sure children are protected and looked after by their parents, or by other people when this is needed. Governments should make sure that people and places responsible for looking after children are doing a good job.

#12. Children have the right to give their opinions freely on issues that affect them. Adults should listen and take children seriously.

#13. Children have the right to share freely with others what they learn, think and feel, by talking, drawing, writing or in any other way unless it harms other people.

#17. Children have the right to get information from the Internet, radio, television, newspapers, books and other sources. Adults should make sure the information they are getting is not harmful. Governments should encourage the media to share information from lots of different sources, in languages that all children can understand.

#30. Children have the right to use their own language, culture and religion—even if these are not shared by most people in the country where they live.

#31. Every child has the right to rest, relax, play and to take part in cultural and creative activities.

What rights do you believe should exist in a list like the Convention on the Rights of the Child? Make a list.

____

____

____

____

____

____

Do you believe the United States should have our own "Children's Bill of Rights"? Why or why not?

____

____

____

____

Walking the Fine Line

Flint: You mentioned at one point that you had been told to "walk a fine line" by someone at your school, right? Can you tell me what that means? Who told you that?

Katherine: I was told that by my administrator, my principal. She was trying to protect me by saying it, but I don't find it helpful, because it sounds like you're telling me to be careful, and I live my life thinking about how to be careful as a queer person in the Deep South. Counselors are often told, "Do what's right, but keep your job."

Flint: More complicated than it sounds, I think.

Katherine: Right? What happens when "what's right" is what would get me fired? I spent a lot of time in that space. I used to tell myself, sure, maybe that's true, "Do what's right, but keep your job," but the moment that you lean more toward "keep your job" rather than "do what's right," why are you here?

Flint: Oof, that hits you right in the chest.

Katherine: I cannot live like that. I think that standing your ground can be really important in those moments, because I found that the times when I was most scared? When I did stand my ground? People tended to back down. They back off. They wanted to see if I would comply in advance.

Flint: Too see if you were just going to make it easy for them.

Katherine: I think that "walking a fine line" thing comes from a lot of white straight people who live their whole lives thinking, "Well, it's safer for me to not make waves." They haven't had to practice doing hard stuff. They have not had to practice standing up in situations where they're uncomfortable.

They've spent their life practicing "Just look away" or "Just don't say anything." But when you're queer, when you're Black, when you're Hispanic, when you're trans, you grow up asking "Am I gonna self-deny? Am I gonna just hush and fall back and have another piece of me break off? Or am I gonna get brave?"

Flint: Right.

Katherine: So many well-meaning straight people have told me "Don't make this harder for yourself," but I've never regretted the hard-for-myself thing. I have certainly regretted fading into the background and keeping quiet and just letting something pass.

Reflect for a moment on the advice "Do what's right, but keep your job." Is there truth within it? Why or why not?

____

____

____

____

Let's Recap:

What sticks out to you about Katherine's experiences? What are your overall reflections for this chapter?

____

____

____

____

What questions do you still have?

____

____

Teaching Like. . .Theresa

Pre-Quiz[41]

1. Despite some assumptions about crime rates within the United States, the number of incarcerated youth has been dropping steadily for decades. By what percentage has the number of youth held in juvenile justice facilities fallen since 2000?[42]
   A. 30%
   B. 52%
   C. 68%
   D. 74%
2. West Virginia (245 per 100,000), Alaska (210 per 100,000), and Louisiana (158 per 100,000) have the highest youth incarceration rate of any other US state. New Jersey, however, has one of the lowest. What is the youth incarceration rate in New Jersey?
   A. 87 per 100,000
   B. 46 per 100,000
   C. 20 per 100,000
   D. 8 per 100,000
3. Though they make up just over 10% of the student population, what percentage of LGBTQ+ youth between the ages of 13 and 17 report experiencing school discipline of some sort, such as suspension or expulsion?[43]
   A. 15%
   B. 20%
   C. 25%
   D. 33%
4. According to the US Trans Survey, 72% of adult respondents reported that they would be "somewhat" or "very" uncomfortable with *what*?
   A. Asking for help from law enforcement
   B. Using a public restroom
   C. Reaching out to a friend for advice
   D. Speaking at a public event

[41] Answer Key: 1. D, 2. B, 3. D, 4. A.

[42] Rovner, Joshua. "Youth Justice by the Numbers." The Sentencing Project, 14 Aug 2024, www.sentencingproject.org/policy-brief/youth-justice-by-the-numbers/.

[43] Nittle, Nadra. "LGBTQ+ Students Face Disproportionately High Rates of Discipline in Schools, Research Shows." The 19th, 30 June 2022, 19thnews.org/2022/06/lgbtq-students-discipline-schools-supportive-leadership/.

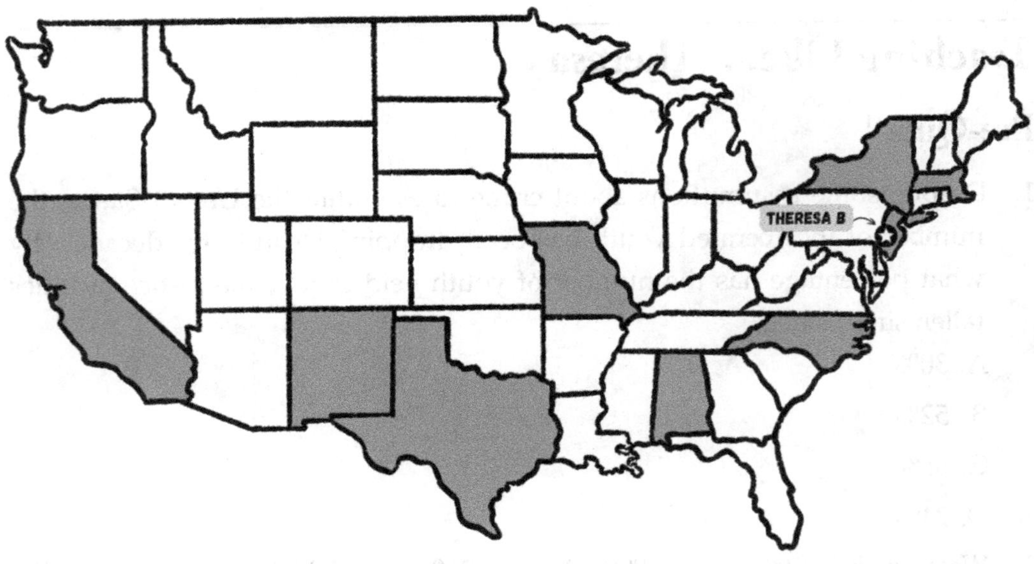

Theresa B (she/her)
New Jersey
Juvenile Detention Center Principal

Theresa, the principal of the education department at a juvenile detention center in New Jersey, began her career as an English teacher in a more "traditional" high school before pivoting to an environment most families hope their children will never encounter. "A lot of people are terrified of these kids," she says, and she knows just how high the deck is stacked against them. Of the more-or-less 48 minors between grades 6 and 12 in her care (the number changes daily as children are shuffled through courts and other facilities), Theresa believes in the future of every single one. "Our kids are colossally underserved," she says. "I love them, and I want them to love themselves."

Based on your knowledge and/or assumptions about LGBTQ+ acceptance and protections in New Jersey, as well as your knowledge and/or assumptions about the student population within juvenile detention, what are some of your worries, concerns, and hopes for Theresa's experience?

____

____

____

____

____

____

In what ways do you identify with Theresa? How are your experiences in education similar? How are they different?

____

____

____

____

> Content warning: in this chapter, Theresa shares stories of incarcerated queer children, and many of them may be hard to read. Please practice care with yourself moving forward from here, as some of these stories feature mentions of violence, prostitution,[44] and suicide.

A Whole Other Level of Trauma

Flint: So, this is a really unfamiliar area for me. What would you consider to be some of the primary differences between a more traditional high school and where you are now?

Theresa: Well, I'm in a detention center, so the students are housed here while they are waiting for the judge to decide on their case, or they're waiting for their next court date. They're in jail, so they're not given free rein: they're told when to get up, what underwear to wear—they have so many more issues to deal with than kids in a "regular" school district.

Flint: It's hard to even know how to begin to imagine that.

[44] I have gone back and forth about the language used in this chapter, and I have decided to keep the original word used by the interviewee: "prostitution." Though I am of the opinion that the word describing "prostitution of a minor" is more accurately "trafficking," as a child cannot consent to sex work, only 30 US states (including Washington DC) have protective laws preventing children from being arrested for solicitation. New Jersey does not have these protections, so the language will stand as a reminder of the many ways our laws continue to fail children. To learn more about child trafficking within the United States, visit www.love146.org.

Theresa: **There are so many questions for them, like "Who's being taken care of at home?" and "Has mom been able to pay the bills?" Is the judge going to be lenient, or is the judge going to send them away for two years this time, instead of letting them go home on the electronic monitor and bracelet?**

There's also a whole other level of trauma that they have experienced throughout their lives before they've even gotten here. My kids are predominantly from [city], which is a place without a lot of resources. They don't have a lot of people advocating for them, and most are coming from poverty. We sometimes get the children and grandchildren of former residents, so it really is this cycle that they're stuck in. No one's shown them a different way of life.

What about the environment of juvenile detention complicates the work of education and advocacy? What do you imagine are some major hurdles of that work? What questions do you have as you continue from here?

____

____

____

____

____

____

A Different Type of Person

Theresa: **In my time here, we've only had one student who was a trans girl. She went by Alexis,[45] and thank God they housed her with the female residents, because that's a safety issue. She had long hair, and she was beautiful and funny, but we would still have officers who would. . . [hesitates].**

Flint: It's okay, take your time.

Theresa: **Well. . .my principal told me a long time ago—the woman I replaced—she told me, "Honey, the type of person who joins law enforcement? The type of person who becomes a juvenile**

[45] Name has been changed.

detention officer or wants to be a corrections officer? That's a different type of person than someone who wants to become an educator." She told me, "They're not going to get it—they don't care the way you care."

Flint: I think that's true, yeah.

Theresa: So, yes, Alexis was in the girl unit, but officers would sometimes still call her [deadname].

Flint: They would intentionally misgender her.

Theresa: 100%. Yes.

Flint: In your facility, how many students are in your care?

Theresa: Right now, we have 48. It changes daily really. But I think we're capped at either 50 or 60. We can't have more than that.

Flint: And how many corrections officers?

Theresa: I think each division has 15 officers, one for each unit. Right now, we have seven units. They might have a couple of floaters who will be responsible for the entire day for bringing kids to appointments, because they have to literally walk the kid from place to place. We also have an officer up in central control who has all the monitors and has to unlock the doors for people when they're leaving secure areas. So, 15 might be a high estimate.

Flint: But either way, that's like a one-to-five, right? That's a better ratio than any educational facility in the country for any kind of classroom aide or helper.

Theresa: Right.

Flint: So, for the officer who is intentionally misgendering Alexis, what's the dynamic of that for the educators in the building? Do you talk to them about it?

Theresa: As far as I know, when [the officers] were speaking about Alexis, it never happened in my presence or in the presence of any of the other teachers. Down in the unit—that's the housing unit—after school, that's where a lot of hanging out happens. That's when a lot of—truth be told—not great things happen. That's when a lot of fights happen. There are fewer witnesses.

Flint: Cameras?

Theresa: **There are cameras, but none of them is miked. If someone's going to be an ass to you, they're probably going to be smart about it and do it where "It's your word against mine."**

Flint: That's such a frustrating dynamic.

Theresa: **There have been situations where, depending on who the officer is, kids have been provoked into lashing out. If you have the wrong personality with you for 12 hours a day—because the shift for officers is 7 a.m. to 7 p.m. and then 7 p.m. to 7 a.m.—if you've got an officer with you for the whole day who you know doesn't respect you. . .If a kid is disrespectful or if a kid curses, they can be punished and have privileges taken away if their behavior is viewed as disrespectful toward the officer. It's this terrible imbalance of power.**

What are your initial thoughts and feelings about the role of corrections officers within juvenile detention?

____

____

Take a moment to reflect on the words of Theresa's predecessor: ". . .the type of person who joins law enforcement? The type of person who becomes a juvenile detention officer or wants to be a corrections officer? That's a different type of person than someone who wants to become an educator." What do you think she means? Do you agree with her? Why or why not?

____

____

____

____

How might the "imbalance of power" Theresa describes more acutely impact queer children living within juvenile detention?

____

____

____

____

We Were His Family

Theresa: **I've had one particular student at the top of my mind...**

Flint: Please, yeah, tell me about them.

Theresa: **Xavier[46] lost his mom when he was five, she died of an overdose, and his father also struggled with addiction. I don't know how much support he ever got with his identity. I saw some pictures recently of Xavier with his mom when he was really young, and—from the jump—it was obvious; that's not [deadname], that's Xavier. It was strange to see him with long hair and in a dress, because you could even tell at that age—that child was uncomfortable.**

Flint: [laughs] Yeah, I can relate to that.

Theresa: **Mom was very supportive, though. She referred to her kid as a "tomboy," but I think mom was as supportive as she could be, but I don't think Xavier received that kind of support after she passed. There were issues of neglect, to the point where Xavier was a big behavior problem in school. And he had, I think, mental health struggles.**

Flint: That sounds familiar too.

Theresa: **Yeah, Xavier was lashing out, but he was incredibly bright. Dad withdrew him from school and was supposed to set him up with online school, but never did. He ended up coming here when he was 14.**

Flint: Wow.

Theresa: **We didn't have records for school past the fourth grade for him, and there was a whole bunch going on in addition to that. We found out that Xavier had been prostituting himself in [city] for drugs. There was substance abuse and just a whole lot of really dangerous behavior.**

Just being in the child's presence, I felt a weight. How do you recover from any of these pieces that you have going on in your life? Any of these pieces would be enough to break somebody.

Flint: Do you remember why he first came in?

---

[46] Name has been changed.

Theresa: **I don't remember what Xavier's initial charges were, no, but he was with us for a while. He did have grandparents who were very supportive of him, but Dad refused to give over any sort of custody. Dad wouldn't answer our calls or appear in court. Grandmom really wanted to be there and support Xavier, but Dad wouldn't let her.**

Flint: I'm sure the family dynamics are extra complicated within this system.

Theresa: **Yeah, there was so much. Sometimes what kids will do when they're afraid to leave is they will create a situation in which they think a judge will keep them here. And so Xavier assaulted a couple officers, and one of them was a friend of mine. She said, "He body slammed me, man." And Xavier was not a big kid, but he had some strength to him.**

Flint: So did he get sent away?

Theresa: **Well, Xavier did leave, but then he ran from that program and came back. The last time we had him, the court released Xavier to his dad.**

Flint: Oh no.

Theresa: **Yep. He slashed all of his dad's tires and tried to set fire to his dad's house.**

Flint: Wow.

Theresa: **And before he was picked up again, he got an Uber to [city] and walked out onto a bridge.**

And then he jumped.

We attended his funeral last month, and the only thing that brought me peace was remembering that there was so much on this child's plate, but now he's free and hopefully at peace. And if there's an afterlife, maybe his mom was there, who he clearly loved and who clearly loved him, even though she struggled with her own issues.

Flint: Thank you for sharing his life with us.

Theresa: **Last month, when we were at the service, his grandmother came over to us and said that Xavier, on more than one occasion, said that the people here. . .we were his family.**

Flint: I'm sure. Thank you.

Instead of answering specific questions for this segment, take a moment to write a letter to Xavier, or to any other kid who has been robbed of the childhood they deserve.

The "What Ifs"

Flint: How do you carry that heaviness around? You said this funeral was a month ago, and you're still here. You're showing up to work. This is above and beyond what most educators put themselves through.

Theresa: **It sounds corny, but I truly believe this: I'm honored to know each and every one of these kids. These are kids who people are afraid of, who people hate, who people fear, who people don't want anything to do with. Schools don't want these kids. We are given this opportunity to know them. It's tragic what happened with Xavier, but on the flip side, I think, "Thank God he was with us for the time that he was. Thank God he had the experience of people honoring who he was." For a while, he was safe, and he had three meals a day, and he wasn't having to prostitute himself.**

Flint: He had some love and consistency.

Theresa: **I don't want to waste my energy on "what ifs" when it could be better served making these kids feel seen and loved and shown that they're worthy of an education. They deserve someone sitting down next to them and asking them questions about themselves and making an effort to get to know them. So, yeah, that's how I do it. Because I love these kids.**

Flint: You love these kids.

Theresa: **And I think a lot of other people don't. They don't want them. I feel like it's an honor to work with them, all the kids here, even though some of them are huge pains in the ass.**

Flint: [laughs]

Theresa: [laughs]

Flint: And really, thank you. This is one of those jobs that I think a lot of teachers would never even consider.

Theresa: Right.

Flint: I mean even just middle school is already a really tough thing to ask of a teacher. To add all of this extra shit is. . .

Theresa: When I hire teachers or instructional assistants, it's almost immediately clear whether they're gonna make it or not. You're going to be told to "Go f*ck yourself" in 14 different ways. Whatever physical insecurities you didn't have, you're going to have now. They find shit, they will find whatever your insecurities are and capitalize on them.

Flint: You have to be an extra tough cookie.

Theresa: But the people who stay, stay. Our history teacher has been here since 1989.

Flint: Woo! Okay.

Theresa: A bunch of our other teachers have been here since the early 2000s. I knew when I started here, maybe three months in, that I wasn't going anywhere. This is where I want to be. So conversely, it's very apparent who's a good fit.

Flint: It sounds like a teacher who can last here is someone who's thick-skinned, right? But also, it sounds like, you have to have a huge amount of love for the kids in your care.

Theresa: They also have to be able to build rapport and to have a relationship with a struggling kid. Some days I'll say, "I get it, you don't feel like doing math today. Let's just sit together, we'll do these two problems together, and then you can chill out."

Flint: In some ways it's an entirely different world, but there's a lot that feels so familiar too.

Theresa: And there's never a perfect answer. Some of the kids are going to be away for a really long time, so sometimes they'll say, "What does this matter?" and I'll have to say to them, "I can't say that I would think any differently if I were you in your situation right now, but my hope is that someday you come around and think of yourself as the smart and capable person that you are and that you want to do this for yourself. I hope, eventually, you want to get your diploma for yourself."

In what way is teaching within a juvenile detention facility similar to teaching in a more "traditional" setting? How is it different?

____

____

____

____

After seeing Theresa's description of the kind of teacher who "lasts" in this environment, do you think you could see yourself working in a position such as hers? Why or why not?

____

____

____

____

Let's Recap:

What sticks out to you about Theresa's experiences? What are your overall reflections for this chapter?

____

____

____

____

What questions do you still have?

____

____

Teaching Like. . .Ro and Alaina

Pre-Quiz[47]

1. The Stonewall National Monument, the site of the 1969 Stonewall riots that sparked a new era for the LGBTQ+ rights movement across the United States, has been the center of what recent controversy at the hands of the federal government?
   A. The removal of the site's LGBTQ+ pride flag
   B. The removal of "transgender" from the National Park Service website's page for the Stonewall National Monument
   C. The removal of "gay" from the National Park Service website's page for the Stonewall National Monument
   D. All of the above
   E. Both A and B
2. Approximately how many LGBTQ+ residents live within the New York metro area?
   A. 100,000
   B. 250,000
   C. 500,000
   D. 700,000
3. What American political organization began as a movement against COVID-19 mask and vaccine mandates in schools but pivoted to anti-LGBTQ+ efforts and book banning in 2022?
   A. Turning Point USA
   B. Moms for Liberty
   C. Focus on the Family
   D. The Westboro Baptist Church
4. Featuring a student population of just over 100 and a staff of 15, what is the name of the Manhattan public high school designed specifically for (though not limited to) the needs of LGBTQ+ young people in New York City?
   A. Sylvia Rivera High School
   B. Harvey Milk High School
   C. Marsha P. Johnson High School
   D. Stormé DeLarverie High School

[47] Answer Key: 1. E, 2. D, 3. B, 4. B.

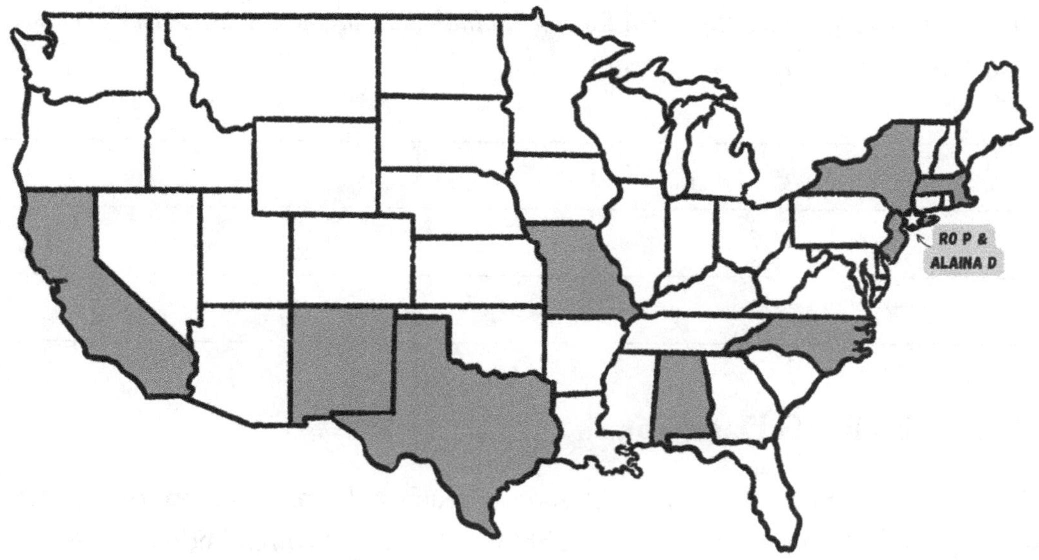

Ro Peña (they/them) and **Alaina Daniels** (she/they)
New York
Founders of Trans formative Schools

Ro and Alaina are the founders of Trans formative Schools (TfS), a free after-school program built to serve the needs of trans and nonbinary 9- to 15-year-olds in New York City. "What we're doing is designed to bring together educators, researchers, organizers, youth, and families to generate trans knowledge and to build trans power," says Alaina. "The after-school space is our pilot program. The next step is a full-day tuition-free middle school." The teachers and young people of TfS were Grand Marshals of the 2025 NYC Pride Parade, and they have their sights set on continuing to grow and empower trans youth and educators alike. "We're trying to center joy as best we can," says Ro, "We want to make sure that people know that we exist."

Based on your knowledge and/or assumptions about LGBTQ+ acceptance and protections in New York, what are some of your worries, concerns, and hopes for the experiences of both Ro and Alaina?

____

____

____

____

In what ways do you identify with Ro and Alaina? How are your experiences in education similar? How are they different?

____

____

____

____

"Your Teacher Is Dangerous"

Flint: Both of you were classroom teachers before you founded Trans formative schools, right? What is it that compelled you to leave and start something new together?

Ro: **Well, I was working at a progressive private school on the Upper West Side of Manhattan, and that's where I met Alaina. I'd been working there seven or eight years, and I was able to tailor my classroom into a space that felt pretty closely aligned to who I am as a nonbinary, brown, fat, and very vocal person. There was a good amount of freedom for children to express themselves in authentic ways without adult supremacy taking over the classroom, so I did have a lot of liberties teaching kids in affinity spaces: queer affinity spaces, Black and Brown affinity spaces, Latinx affinity spaces. . .**

Flint: That sounds like the dream, but I have a feeling there's a turn coming.

Ro: **Yeah, because still within that, there were moments where I didn't feel fully supported, didn't feel fully seen, and didn't feel fully liberated in the ways that I needed as a person. And so, I decided to leave [school] and pivot. I was going to spend a year figuring out what to do, but then Alaina floated this idea that they had been developing with a different educator. I said, "Let me think on it," and then almost immediately I said, "I've got to meet with them," and so I did. And it felt great. It felt purposeful. It felt exactly like what I needed. And now, I think, this is a good time for Alaina to jump in.**

Flint: Enter Alaina!

Alaina: **Well, I too spent over a decade teaching, but mostly in middle school and some high school. I've taught science, activism, sex ed, robotics, engineering, frisbee, roller skating, and I've been a lunch lady. This is mostly within progressive private, but also some public, schools.**

Flint: Roller skating?

Alaina: **Yeah, we'd skate the loop in Central Park.**

Flint: That's incredible.

Alaina: **And I transitioned in the classroom. I came out my second and third year teaching.**

Flint: How was that?

Alaina: **The kids were fabulous. The adults were complicated. This is at what, I would argue, is the most progressive school east of California. The students would do an activism project every year. One year we did Syrian refugees. One year we did sexual assault on college campuses. One year we did the school-to-prison pipeline. The students would pick [the topic], and we would spend a year learning and then doing activism to try and change stuff.**

Flint: Wow.

Alaina: **So yeah, even there, the first 20 adults I said something to about my transition all asked some version of "Are you going to have *the surgery*?"**

Flint: That's gross.

Alaina: **As a trans woman teacher, there are a lot of assumptions that trans women are dangerous for kids. When I would lead a field trip, there would be multiple randos coming up to kids saying, "Your teacher's a man and is dangerous." Sometimes they were just trolls, but a lot of times, they were a parent or an elder, or somebody who was genuinely concerned for the kids. If you are a trans seventh grader watching your trans woman teacher deal with this? We had community meetings about it, but five years later [the school] still couldn't get my name and pronouns right, so I left.**

Both Ro and Alaina make a point to mention that the discrimination, harassment, and hardships they experienced as trans teachers occurred within progressive private schools. What's the purpose of this choice, do you think?

____

____

____

____

Ro and Alaina left more traditional roles in education to start an after-school program for trans youth. What do you think a program like theirs should offer? What, from your perspective, do young trans people need that most schools are unable to provide?

____

____

____

____

Responding to Unmet Needs

Alaina: **TfS came out of both Ro's and my unmet needs, as well as the kids' unmet needs. There are not a lot of trans teachers, and the only trans women of color teachers that I've known? They've all left the profession.**

Flint: What are some of those needs, do you think? How are you meeting them?

Ro: **Okay, so, I'll tell you a story. At this last school, my administrators got an email from a mom who was very upset, because her son reported that I made students do pronoun songs every morning.**

Flint: Pronoun songs?

Ro: **Yeah, so, one: untrue. But also, that sounds so fun, right? A pronoun song every morning? The whole time I am reading this email, I'm thinking, "Wait, what's the problem?" But it was untrue. This parent got really upset because she was stuck on this idea that I was only talking about gender in my classroom, and gender was the "thing" I was about. And here I am, mostly excited to learn about the fish of the Hudson River.**

Flint: [laughs]

Ro: So, this mom tried to rally grown-ups against me, but at least it backfired, because the other grown-ups said, "Hold on, we're not against Ro at all. We just want more information." Her whole plan fell apart very quickly. But it exposed something else for me: I wasn't informed directly that any of this was happening. The school wasn't like, "Hey, Ro, just so you know, this happened last week, and we want to give you information about it." They didn't CC me in the email. They didn't do anything to say, "We immediately have your back, because we believe you and we've seen you teach."

Flint: That's so disappointing.

Ro: That's what it is. All of these little stories compounded to the point where I was so tired. I loved working there, I truly did. I met beautiful people who are my besties to this day. And yet, I couldn't go on. I needed something different, and I needed something that felt more whole and supportive than what I was experiencing there.

Flint: And these are needs that are met in this new space?

Ro: Personally, my needs are being met because I get to teach trans kids and I get to be in classrooms with other trans adults, and it is this beautiful constellation of queer babies having hard, challenging dialogues, or having really fun and fruitful conversations. All of that is happening every day, Monday through Thursday, 2:30 to 5:30, in our tiny little classroom.

Flint: This is after school, four days a week. Are the kids from schools across the city?

Ro: Yes, and a lot of our students choose not to go to school anymore physically, so many of them are homeschooled. And, unfortunately, some of our students have left the country this year or have had to move from Florida to here. We're navigating holding space for students who might not be able to show up all the time because of the litany of things that have happened to them.

Flint: That's a lot of heaviness to unpack with them.

Ro: We just had a rally for trans youth this past Saturday, and a lot of our kids got an opportunity to talk and voice their own opinions about what's been happening. My goal is to shut the f*ck up and let kids lead. When they need assistance, we just whisper guidance in the background.

Alaina mentions that all of the "trans women of color teachers" she's known have "left the profession." What are some reasons why longevity might decrease when a teacher exists within multiple marginalized identities?

___

___

___

___

Educators aren't often encouraged to consider our own needs within the classroom. What are some needs that we're told to ignore or devalue in the service of our profession and the needs of our students?

___

___

___

___

Ro is not the first educator within this workbook who has lamented a lack of support from their administrators. What can "higher-ups" within a district or school community do to better support the trans teachers working within their classrooms?

___

___

___

___

Critiquing and Building

Alaina: **Something I know I can do is build a space that can handle conflict and repair. I did it in my classroom, and what we've been learning over the last three or four years is how to create that on a school level, on a coalition level, and then hopefully, on a larger community level.**

Flint: Wait, say more about that.

Alaina: **Well, there is a big difference between *critiquing* and *building*. Critiquing is saying, "This is not safe enough. This is hurtful. This is harmful." And I think we live in a world where the history of white supremacist colonization is never going to end. It's never going away. It exists. It happened. Do I dream of a world where we're all free? Yes. But *building* is the thing that can get us there. That's what TfS is trying to do. Our big, long-term, two decades, three decades goal, is a movement of trans schools.**

Flint: That's the plan for the future?

Alaina: **Think Montessori or Catholic or charter, or schools for the deaf, schools for the blind, HBCUs—any movement of schools. We partnered early with Mocha Celis, a trans school based in Buenos Aires, and co-presented together at the second International Trans Conference at Northwestern. They're building a network of trans schools in Argentina. Folks keep telling us that we should be bragging that we're the first trans school, but trans schools have existed throughout history. Marsha P. Johnson and Sylvia Rivera, with STAR,[48] started a trans school three blocks from where I sit. It only lasted a year and a half, but they started a school.**

Were you familiar with the history and contemporary existence of transgender-specific schools, both within the United States and internationally? Why or why not?

____

____

____

____

What, from your perspective, would be necessary to make a trans-specific school effective? Why?

____

____

____

____

[48] Street Transvestite Action Revolutionaries (STAR).

When Children Speak

Alaina: **Our local school board, the school board for Stonewall, has been taken over by Moms for Liberty. They've been pushing a strong right-wing agenda, including trying to ban the books written by our founding board chair, Dr. Megan Madison, because they tell true stories about race and gender and justice and consent and ability and power. The board is also coming after the guidelines for trans kids that I helped write.**

Flint: That's a lot to take on.

Alaina: **And when they passed attacks on trans girls playing sports, Chase Strangio,[49] who was working alongside us, he said, "If you pass this, we'll be back next month with more people, and back the next month after that with more people, and back the next month after that with more people." And that's what we did. We've been back every month with more people. After 18 months, we got them to rescind it. And that is, to brag, skilled organizing.**

Flint: I'd say so, yeah.

Ro: **There are students who are selected to sit on the school board, and they don't get a vote; they just have to sit there and listen to all these grown-ups vote about their rights, which makes absolutely no sense. And last year, it was very clear that these kids would have voted to support rescinding Resolution 248,[50] but they simply weren't allowed to vote. But they did use their platform to speak out for trans youth. Our mission this year is to ensure that these kids, whoever they are, get the opportunity to speak.**

Flint: That's huge. So much of this kind of organizing, it sounds, is an exercise in stamina. Is that right?

Alaina: **I think stamina is part of it, but I also think that strategy is another big part.**

Flint: Tell me about that.

Alaina: **The strategy and tactics and approach to organizing was developed over generations by Black organizers, primarily at**

[49] Chase Strangio is an American lawyer and trans activist famous for being the first known transgender person to make oral arguments before the Supreme Court.

[50] The school district's trans sports ban.

organizations based in the south. Dr. Megan has been teaching that to us, and we've been passing that mentorship down. Part of what TfS is designed to do is teach trans people organizing. I thought I was a good organizer, and it's turned out that I actually didn't know shit.

Flint: [laughs]

Alaina: In some ways it's about building power. Some of it's about developing a strategy for figuring out what you want. Some is then about using smart tactics to get there. If we want the students on the school board to be allowed to vote, we have to ask, who is it that can give us that? What tactics can we use to get them to vote the way we want?

Flint: And what does that look like?

Alaina: Well, we looked at the 12 members of the school board and figured out who the three swing votes were, and then we spent 18 months trying different experiments to see what would persuade them. Ro gave them flowers. We all danced the Macarena and "Hot to Go." We brought signs. We did fact checks. We had folks do silent mime mockery of various folks. We wrote collective testimony. We dressed in all white. We dressed in all black. We dressed in rainbow.

Flint: Wow.

Ro: We had children speak.

Alaina: We had children speak. And when the school board members were evil, and when the trolls showed up and said hateful stuff, a bunch of the kids left the room in tears. So we stopped. We're careful with when we put the kids out there. I tell them, "It's not your job to have to lead." They should get to just be kids and not have to, you know, be leading a protest movement. But if they want to lead, I'll follow their lead. And Ro does such a great job helping them figure out what they want to say.

Flint: Yeah?

Ro: I hate editing kids' conversations, so I try not to. They're so authentic, and that's something that their grown-ups are learning about. Obviously, they want their kids to do well on the stand, but you know, at the end of the day, these kids are going to say everything that needs to be said.

What is your take on Ro and Alaina's strategy for organizing?

____

____

____

____

Alaina says that they are careful about when they center the kids of Trans formative Schools in organizing efforts. What are the pros and cons of allowing children the space to be heard in public forums? What are the dangers of creating that space and the dangers of limiting it?

____

____

____

____

Let's Recap:

What sticks out to you about Ro and Alaina's experiences? What are your overall reflections for this chapter?

____

____

____

____

What questions do you still have?

____

____

SECTION THREE

Wrapping Up. . .

CHAPTER SIX

Ending Quiz: Are You Teaching Like an Ally?

Welcome to the end of *The Teach Like an Ally Workbook*, which means it's time for us to revisit the quiz that launched us into this journey together: *Are You Teaching Like an Ally?* Try not to flip back and check your answers or your original score as you take on this quiz again—go with your gut, and let this be the same kind of reflective tool as it was when you began. LGBTQ+ allyship work isn't a race.

Like I said at the start, this quiz is *not a* ***sentencing***. *It's a* ***starting point***, even now. Let this be a tool to guide your self-reflection, not override it. The questions here are meant to allow you a shot at personal vulnerability, and we are all starting from different blocks.

Now is the time to ask: where have you been able to **build your confidence**? What gaps in your knowledge or perspective found the space to be filled? The changes might be **vast** or **immeasurably narrow**, but the truth is the same either way: **the only way to lose is not to try**.

As you answer each question, keep a tally of your points as you go. Each answer is worth either **4, 3, 2, or 1** point(s), and the values **won't be the same** every time. **Double check your math before you visit your results!**

1. I have made mistakes as an ally.
   A. Strongly Agree (4)
   B. Agree (3)
   C. Disagree (2)
   D. Strongly Disagree (1)
2. When I have made a mistake as an ally, I have attempted steps to take accountability and begin repair.
   A. Strongly Agree (4)
   B. Agree (3)

C. Disagree (2)

D. Strongly Disagree (1)

3. When my mistakes are brought to my attention, I try to avoid reacting quickly and defensively.

A. Strongly Agree (4)

B. Agree (3)

C. Disagree (2)

D. Strongly Disagree (1)

4. I see "ally" as a verb and not a noun.

A. Strongly Agree (4)

B. Agree (3)

C. Disagree (2)

D. Strongly Disagree (1)

5. The young people in my life know, because I have told them, that they can come to me when they are feeling unsafe or unsupported.

A. Strongly Agree (4)

B. Agree (3)

C. Disagree (2)

D. Strongly Disagree (1)

6. I try not to challenge the systems and structures of my school and community, as they seem to work well for most people.

A. Strongly Agree (1)

B. Agree (2)

C. Disagree (3)

D. Strongly Disagree (4)

7. There are only one or two staff members in our school community who know about and handle LGBTQ+ issues, and that system works well enough.

A. Strongly Agree (1)

B. Agree (2)

C. Disagree (3)

D. Strongly Disagree (4)

8. When I need to learn about a term, concept, or event in the LGBTQ+ community, I will ask a student first.

   A. Strongly Agree (1)

   B. Agree (2)

   C. Disagree (3)

   D. Strongly Disagree (4)

9. My students can "just tell" that I'm supportive of them, and I don't have to do anything further to be an ally to them.

   A. Strongly Agree (1)

   B. Agree (2)

   C. Disagree (3)

   D. Strongly Disagree (4)

10. Sitting in discomfort and challenging my belief systems is part of allyship work.

    A. Strongly Agree (4)

    B. Agree (3)

    C. Disagree (2)

    D. Strongly Disagree (1)

11. If I hold a marginalized identity, I am automatically an ally to my students and do not have to do anything further to be an ally to them.

    A. Strongly Agree (1)

    B. Agree (2)

    C. Disagree (3)

    D. Strongly Disagree (4)

12. If none of my students or colleagues tells me that they are part of the LGBTQ+ community, it's unlikely that any of them are.

    A. Strongly Agree (1)

    B. Agree (2)

    C. Disagree (3)

    D. Strongly Disagree (4)

13. When I look at the list of terms within the LGBTQ+ Terminology page, I can say with confidence that I know and can appropriately use at least 75% of them.

    A. Strongly Agree (4)

    B. Agree (3)

C. Disagree (2)

D. Strongly Disagree (1)

14. When someone comes out to me as transgender, I can use the name and pronouns they ask of me with minimal error.

A. Strongly Agree (4)

B. Agree (3)

C. Disagree (2)

D. Strongly Disagree (1)

15. When I do make a name or pronoun error, I correct myself quickly and without fanfare.

A. Strongly Agree (4)

B. Agree (3)

C. Disagree (2)

D. Strongly Disagree (1)

16. When someone I know uses the pronouns "they/them," I know how to fit them into sentences quickly and with minimal error.

A. Strongly Agree (4)

B. Agree (3)

C. Disagree (2)

D. Strongly Disagree (1)

17. When discussing a trans person's past, I know to keep their name and pronouns congruent with their current lived reality, even if they may have gone by a different name or used different pronouns in the time period of my story. I can do this with minimal error.

A. Strongly Agree (4)

B. Agree (3)

C. Disagree (2)

D. Strongly Disagree (1)

18. I am familiar with many important historical events within the timeline of US LGBTQ+ history (the Stonewall Riots, the AIDS Epidemic, the election and assassination of Harvey Milk, the Lavender Scare) and make an active effort to expand my knowledge where I can.

A. Strongly Agree (4)

B. Agree (3)

C. Disagree (2)

D. Strongly Disagree (1)

19. I consider myself an advanced learner in the world of national and international LGBTQ+ cultural, social, and/or political history, and could likely teach others.
    A. Strongly Agree (4)
    B. Agree (3)
    C. Disagree (2)
    D. Strongly Disagree (1)
20. I avoid gendered language and assumptions within my classroom and school community, such as "I need a couple of boys to help me with these desks" and "Let's make this game boys versus girls."
    A. Strongly Agree (4)
    B. Agree (3)
    C. Disagree (2)
    D. Strongly Disagree (1)
21. "Gender" is a recent issue in schools, and it hasn't been a problem in the past.
    A. Strongly Agree (1)
    B. Agree (2)
    C. Disagree (3)
    D. Strongly Disagree (4)
22. Staff training concerning LGBTQ+ school equity should be optional.
    A. Strongly Agree (1)
    B. Agree (2)
    C. Disagree (3)
    D. Strongly Disagree (4)
23. There is room within my classroom or school community for students to make mistakes, and there are no expectations of perfection.
    A. Strongly Agree (4)
    B. Agree (3)
    C. Disagree (2)
    D. Strongly Disagree (1)
24. I do not apologize to my students.
    A. Strongly Agree (1)
    B. Agree (2)
    C. Disagree (3)
    D. Strongly Disagree (4)

25. I am hard on myself and try for perfection.
    A. Strongly Agree (1)
    B. Agree (2)
    C. Disagree (3)
    D. Strongly Disagree (4)
26. IEPS, 504s, and other accommodation plans are inconvenient and often unnecessary for student success.
    A. Strongly Agree (1)
    B. Agree (2)
    C. Disagree (3)
    D. Strongly Disagree (4)
27. I know that issues of equity across identities, including neurodivergence, race, ethnicity, socioeconomic status, and disability, are tied together in their efforts and purpose, and they can not be treated as separate in the fight for LGBTQ+ liberation.
    A. Strongly Agree (4)
    B. Agree (3)
    C. Disagree (2)
    D. Strongly Disagree (1)
28. I know where the closest community LGBTQ+ Center is located, along with what relevant services and programming might be helpful for my students and colleagues.
    A. Strongly Agree (4)
    B. Agree (3)
    C. Disagree (2)
    D. Strongly Disagree (1)
29. I am familiar with the concept of "rainbow washing," and I know how to prevent it within my own classroom or school community.
    A. Strongly Agree (4)
    B. Agree (3)
    C. Disagree (2)
    D. Strongly Disagree (1)

30. I am familiar with the concepts of "emotional safety" and "psychological safety," and I am confident that my classroom and/or school community promotes both.
    A. Strongly Agree (4)
    B. Agree (3)
    C. Disagree (2)
    D. Strongly Disagree (1)
31. I agree with the phrase "a good teacher is like a candle—it consumes itself to light the way for others."
    A. Strongly Agree (1)
    B. Agree (2)
    C. Disagree (3)
    D. Strongly Disagree (4)
32. I try not to hold children accountable for my feelings. It is my responsibility to regulate myself before engaging with a dysregulated student.
    A. Strongly Agree (4)
    B. Agree (3)
    C. Disagree (2)
    D. Strongly Disagree (1)
33. It is sometimes appropriate to use shame as a teaching strategy.
    A. Strongly Agree (1)
    B. Agree (2)
    C. Disagree (3)
    D. Strongly Disagree (4)
34. I am familiar with the "paradox of tolerance," and I know that I cannot establish a "safe enough" space for LGBTQ+ students within one.
    A. Strongly Agree (4)
    B. Agree (3)
    C. Disagree (2)
    D. Strongly Disagree (1)
35. The policies of my classroom or school community are constructed for the safety and best outcomes of my students, not from my own need for control.
    A. Strongly Agree (4)
    B. Agree (3)

C. Disagree (2)

D. Strongly Disagree (1)

36. The physical environment of my classroom or school community sends a message to LGBTQ+ students and adults that they are safe and respected.

A. Strongly Agree (4)

B. Agree (3)

C. Disagree (2)

D. Strongly Disagree (1)

37. I would support LGBTQ+ students more, but I am concerned that this is "showing a preference" to them and I do not want to appear biased.

A. Strongly Agree (1)

B. Agree (2)

C. Disagree (3)

D. Strongly Disagree (4)

38. I have a strong handle on my values as an educator, and I am willing to stand up for them even if it makes me uncomfortable.

A. Strongly Agree (4)

B. Agree (3)

C. Disagree (2)

D. Strongly Disagree (1)

39. I can spot bullying within my school community, either between students or adults, and I intervene when I see it.

A. Strongly Agree (4)

B. Agree (3)

C. Disagree (2)

D. Strongly Disagree (1)

40. I will challenge teachers, staff, administrators, or other adults within my school community if I see them acting against the interests of LGBTQ+ students and colleagues.

A. Strongly Agree (4)

B. Agree (3)

C. Disagree (2)

D. Strongly Disagree (1)

160–140 points:
You're definitely teaching like an ally, and you're ready to teach others in turn! An expert in the field of LGBTQ+ equity, be proud of what you know and the ways in which you have grown, but don't keep it to yourself! Use your knowledge to enrich your community and help bring other educators up with you. You're killing it!

139–105 points:
You're making major strides to teach like an ally, and you still have room to grow! Though you might not be ready yet to lead a workshop on LGBTQ+ equity, you're putting in the hours and doing an incredible job of expanding your horizons. Keep going!

104–60 points:
You're on board with some of this work, but there are still some gaps in your feelings or understanding, and that's okay! It's hugely impressive to try something new, even if you don't 100% "get it" yet. I'm glad you're here.

59–40 points:
This workbook might not have been the right tool for where you're at in your personal journey to understand and support LGBTQ+ equity, and that's alright! I hope you seek out other voices and continue to learn and grow in your support for the students who need you.

Acknowledgments

Through luck or providence, I ended up interviewing some of the coolest people in the country for this workbook, and I am nothing but humbled and grateful for their contributions. Ro, Alaina, Theresa, Katherine, Janelle, Bali, Matthew, Stanley, Sean Em, I.C., and Mandy: thank you for everything you have done and continue to do for the young people who are lucky enough to end up in your offices and classrooms. Your vulnerability has reminded me that as much as education in our country has continued to break our hearts, our students are worth fighting for, and so are we.

To my husband, Xilo: thank you for convincing me that leaving isn't the same as running away and that we are both worth the comfort and safety we have found in our lives. You are a genius, a marvel, and the kind of partner I didn't know it was possible to deserve.

Bash, Theo, and Max: thank you for lending me your mom again. Jess, one day I will be able to pay you back for the generosity you've shown me through the *two* books we have now worked on together. Your patience, skill, and candor made this book possible.

Finally, I would like to thank the coffee shops and book stores throughout Albuquerque equipped with the trifecta of productivity: comfortable seating, affordable beverages, and accessible wall outlets. Our Airstream has made for a beautiful home but a pretty shitty office. Blackbird Coffee House, Santa Cecilia, and Books on the Bosque: this one's for you.

Acknowledgments

Index

T

U